THE CALL TO CALIFORNIA

THE CAL

TO CALIFORNIA

THE EPIC JOURNEY OF THE PORTOLA-SERRA EXPEDITION IN 1769

A COPLEY BOOK

COMMISSIONED BY JAMES S. COPLEY

CHAIRMAN OF THE CORPORATION THE COPLEY PRESS, INC.

WRITTEN BY RICHARD F. POURADE

EDITOR EMERITUS THE SAN DIEGO UNION

Photography by Harry Crosby

Paintings by Lloyd Harting

PUBLISHED BY THE UNION-TRIBUNE PUBLISHING COMPANY

Contents

Paintings

Dedication

There were men to "match her mountains" and they marched slowly, confidently and courageously into California in 1769.

These were the men under the military leadership of Don Gaspar de Portolá and the spiritual guidance of Father Junípero Serra who won California for the Flag of Castile.

The challenging words of Sam Walter Foss, now chiseled into the marble of California's capitol at Sacramento, reflect upon the exploits of men like Portolá and Serra and express the continuing cry of "Bring me men to match my mountains."

James S. Copley

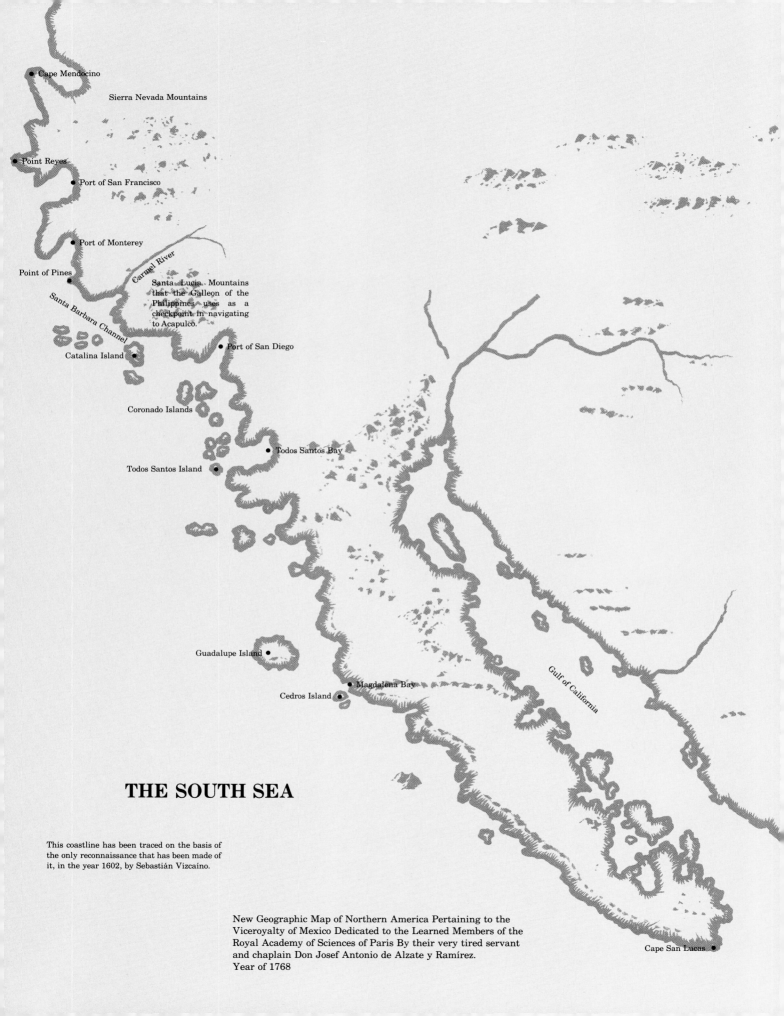

- Cape Mendocino

Sierra Nevada Mountains

- Point Reyes

- Port of San Francisco

- Port of Monterey

Carmel River

Point of Pines

Santa Lucia Mountains that the Galleon of the Philippines uses as a checkpoint in navigating to Acapulco.

Santa Barbara Channel

Catalina Island

- Port of San Diego

Coronado Islands

- Todos Santos Bay

Todos Santos Island

Guadalupe Island

Magdalena Bay

Cedros Island

Gulf of California

THE SOUTH SEA

This coastline has been traced on the basis of the only reconnaissance that has been made of it, in the year 1602, by Sebastián Vizcaíno.

New Geographic Map of Northern America Pertaining to the Viceroyalty of Mexico Dedicated to the Learned Members of the Royal Academy of Sciences of Paris By their very tired servant and chaplain Don Josef Antonio de Alzate y Ramírez.
Year of 1768

Cape San Lucas

the call to California

The Eighteenth Century was beginning to run out. The Spanish Empire was withering away but there would be enough energy left for a few more efforts at colonization.

The English and the French were showing renewed interest in the Pacific and Russia was extending its explorations to the American continent. In January of 1768 the Marques de Grimaldi, Minister of State of Spain, informed the Viceroy of Mexico that Russians had invaded the northwest coast and 300 of them had been slain in an engagement with Indians.

Orders were issued for the occupation of Alta California. It was to be carried out by Spain's traditional means of pacific conquest—the Christianization and civilization of the Indians through the mission system.

At that period the settlements of the Spanish empire in North America extended along a line from the Mississippi River across Texas and New Mexico and into Arizona. Baja California had been occupied for more than seventy years. However, the farthest explorations, those of the Jesuit priest, Father Wenceslaus Link, had not penetrated the interior of the upper third of the peninsula.

Though claimed by Spain, the northwest coast of America had been neglected for a century and a half. By the Spaniards, most of the territory to the north of the settled areas was referred to as California.

The coastline of what is now California was known in a general way from the explorations in 1602 of Sebastián Vizcaíno, who made crude charts of its ports and bestowed names which persisted.

Before him, the coast had been explored by Juan Rodríguez Cabrillo and a number of other Spanish captains.

Also in existence were descriptions of the Pacific Coast written in 1734 by the Pilot Major of the Philippines, Don Joseph Gonzáles Cabrera Bueno, which comprised the sailing directions for pilots of the Manila Galleon.

The Manila Galleon sailed each year between Manila and Acapulco on a Great Circle route which followed the American coast southward to take advantage of favorable currents and prevailing winds.

The Spaniards were secretive about distant possessions and Vizcaíno's charts remained hidden in the archives. A geographic map of 1768 distorted known areas north of Spanish settlements and important coastal points.

This map was printed and circulated freely in Paris and Milan. A partial reproduction with geographic identifications and historic notations in English defines the limits of Spanish explorations of Baja California and the American Far West.

However, the British had learned enough to chart much of what was known as far north as Point Reyes above San Francisco. Some identifications were in error. Vizcaíno's charts and the British map are shown on succeeding pages.

Little was known of the interior of Alta California, however, except of the existence of high mountain ranges often covered with snow visible from the sea.

Thus, with only limited knowledge of the country to the north, and no reliable maps in its possession, an expedition set out for a distant and most legendary land.

PART OF CALIFORNIA

Punta de los Reyes
nes

P.ta de Año Nuevo

P.ta de Pinas

n.ra de la Conceptione

Punta de la Conversion

Farollon de Lobos

S.n Pedro

S.n Bernardo

P.ta de S.n Diego

S.ta Catalina

Ensenada de los Virgines

Isla de S.n Andres

Islas de S.n Martin

I.as de S.n Marcos

Costa Limpia

Baya de S.n Quintin

Cavo Blanco

I. de todas los Santos

Bay de S.n Francisco

Guardaloupe

Isla de Peros

Maria Hermosas

la Assumtion

Los Abrosos

Ensenada de Basos

Farollon de los Alijos

P.ta de N.ra S.ta de los Nubes

Ensenada de Piscador

Cavo S.n Lucas

Las tres Marias

Socoro

Isla de la Passion
discovered in 1715

da

nca Partida

From a high hill at Cape San Lucas, at the tip of Baja California, José de Gálvez watched with satisfaction as the sails of the packetboat *San Antonio,* or *El Príncipe,* as she was commonly known, filled with the wind. She soon disappeared from view in the gathering veil of evening, on her way to Alta California.

The date was February 15, 1769. More than a month before, the packetboat *San Carlos,* or the *El Toyson,* the "Golden Fleece," had put into the bay of La Paz farther up the peninsula on the Gulf of California. There she and her flags had been blessed by Father Junípero Serra. Then she had sailed southward, and rounding the cape, had laid her course for the north.

To Gálvez, Visitor General of New Spain who had been vested with extraordinary powers, the sailing of the two ships, with supplies and soldiers, were the first steps in "putting the lid on California."

A presidio and mission were to be established at the Port of Monterey and a mission at the Port of San Diego. Monterey had been mapped by Vizcaíno and its description given in detail in Cabrera Bueno's sailing directions. In addition, the Carmel River, reported to be an important river in the vicinity of Monterey, was to be explored and possession of the land taken in the name of the King.

It was early in the year and the winds and conditions might not always be favorable for sailing to the north. Gálvez had selected Serra as president of the missions to be established in Alta California but had forbidden him to go by sea. Serra was to go with the land expedition which would meet the two ships at San Diego.

Both ships were of small size for those days. Each was about seventy-two feet in length, and as they had been recently built on the Mexican coast they were not seasoned vessels for so hazardous a journey.

The *San Antonio* carried a crew of twenty-six and two Franciscan padres. The *San Carlos* carried a total of sixty-two persons — a crew of twenty-three and twenty-five Catalan volunteers, and one other padre. A third vessel, the *San José,* was to follow later, but it was delayed time and again.

For many of the members of the land expedition there would be a march of more than a thousand miles. But all leaders, by land and by sea, had been selected because of their knowledge and experience.

Don Gaspar de Portolá, Governor of Baja California, was named commander. He was a captain in the Spanish Dragoons and a soldier of noble birth who had fought well for Spain in Europe.

His second in command, Captain Fernando de Rivera y Moncada, knew the frontier country as he had been a soldier in Baja California for a quarter of a century. The bearded leather-jacket soldiers under him were descendents of people of the frontiers of New Spain.

The Catalan volunteers who were to go by sea were from a Catalonia company of light infantry and had come from Spain in 1767. They were under the command of Lieutenant Don Pedro Fages.

With such diverse backgrounds and experience represented, there would be conflicting counsel in times of stress.

Vicente Vila, in command of the expedition by sea, was a veteran pilot of the Royal Navy. Juan Pérez, in command of the second ship, had been a captain of the Manila Galleon. Miguel Costansó, an army engineer and cosmographer, was going by ship to draw maps and plans of ports to be discovered or occupied. Assigned to join Rivera and take astronomical observations and write the captain's diary was José de Cañizares, a young pilot's mate.

Their positions at various points were to be determined with an astrolabe and a number of members of the expedition were proficient in its use.

Serra himself had been a professor of philosophy at the Franciscan University at Palma on the Mediterranean island of Majorca where he had been born. For nineteen years he had been a missionary in Mexico. One of his former students from Palma, Father Juan Crespí, a tireless traveler, was to keep the official diary of the expedition for the commander.

For about 400 miles north from Loreto, the expedition would follow the trail which had been laid down by the Jesuits during the many years they had established and maintained the missions of Baja California. Today this old trail is almost totally neglected. Modern roads closely parallel it about ten percent of its route, and actually follow it less than five percent. The Jesuits, educated men and breakers of frontiers as well as teachers, had been expelled from Spanish dominions and their missions in Baja California taken over by the Franciscans under Father Serra.

The last mission in their original chain was Santa María, two-thirds of the way up the long, dry and narrow peninsula. Just north of there was a place known as Velicatá. Beyond that point the expedition would be on its own. Rivera was to lead the way, traveling ahead of the second section containing Portolá and Serra, and he was instructed to seek suitable camp and mission sites "to make a ladder to Monterey."

In the early Fall of 1768, members of the land expedition under the direction of Rivera had begun gathering horses, mules and supplies from the lower missions on the peninsula. Serra wrote in his diary that Rivera was to take anything he thought might be useful "and that is what he did; and, although his hand was heavy on the missions, they had to endure it for God and King."

CHAPTER I The Beginning

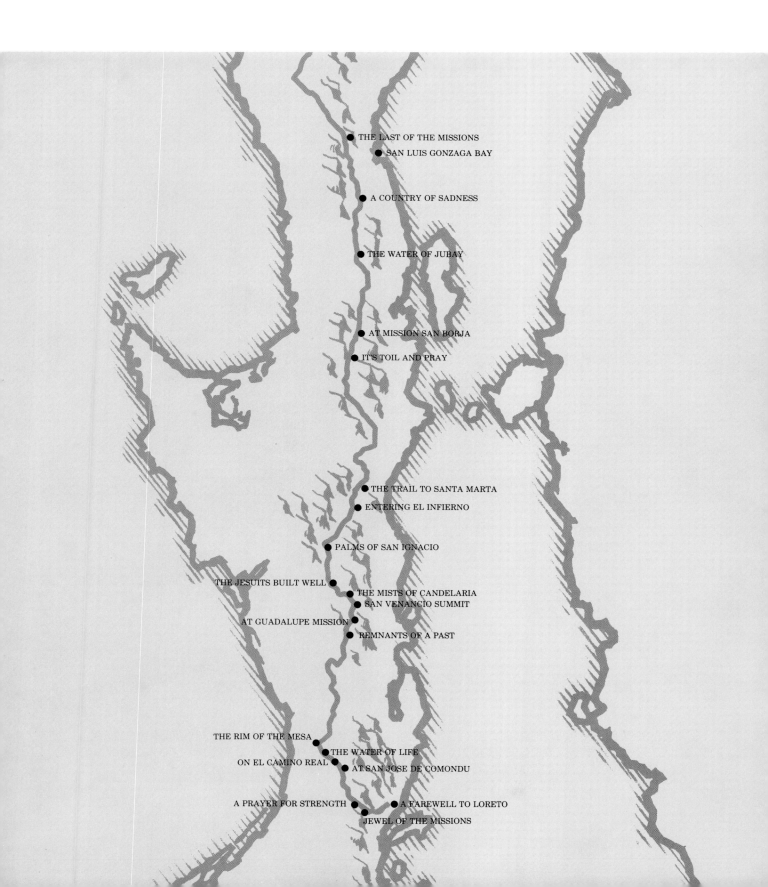

THE LAST OF THE MISSIONS
SAN LUIS GONZAGA BAY

A COUNTRY OF SADNESS

THE WATER OF JUBAY

AT MISSION SAN BORJA
IT'S TOIL AND PRAY

THE TRAIL TO SANTA MARTA
ENTERING EL INFIERNO

PALMS OF SAN IGNACIO

THE JESUITS BUILT WELL
THE MISTS OF CANDELARIA
SAN VENANCIO SUMMIT
AT GUADALUPE MISSION
REMNANTS OF A PAST

THE RIM OF THE MESA
THE WATER OF LIFE
ON EL CAMINO REAL
AT SAN JOSE DE COMONDU

A PRAYER FOR STRENGTH
A FAREWELL TO LORETO
JEWEL OF THE MISSIONS

a farewell to Loreto

From the Presidio and Mission Nuestra Señora de Loreto, which had been his headquarters, Father Junípero Serra rode a mule up into the mountains of Baja California. He was accompanied by a servant and one soldier. The mule was old and broken down, as the best of the mounts had been taken by the military. He was fifty-five years of age. In the forward to his historic diary he wrote:

Of the expedition to the ports of San Diego and Monterey by land, which for God's greater glory and the conversion of the infidels to our Holy Catholic Faith, I began, on March 28, the third day after the feast of Resurrection, in the year 1769, starting from my Mission and the Royal Presidio of Loreto, in California.

From a height on the hills behind Loreto he could look back and see, for the last time, the bay and islands which had become so familiar to him and to so many other Spaniards before him:

I took along no more provisions for so long a journey than a loaf of bread and a piece of cheese, for I was there a whole year, on economic matters, as a mere guest to receive the crumbs of the royal soldier commissioner, whose liberality at my departure did not extend beyond the aforementioned articles.

A leg infection that had pained him since his first days in Mexico would make the trip a difficult one. However, he had told Portolá to start the journey without him, and that he would follow in due time, and "I trust to God that He will give me strength to arrive at San Diego and Monterey."

His trail led up by way of Arroyo de las Parras with its red walls, green palms, cactus and running water, to the peninsular divide at an elevation of 1800 feet, where it turned down a slope into the valley known as San Javier Viejo. There was a mission in San Javier, and though a visit to it would be somewhat out of his way, Serra wanted to say goodby to an old friend and pupil from Majorca, Father Francisco Palóu.

The expedition of which he was the spiritual leader already was stretched out for more than four hundred miles. Months earlier Rivera with twenty-five leather-jacket soldiers and Indian auxiliaries had begun working his way northward, gathering more mules and supplies as he went. Portolá himself had set out with thirty soldiers from Loreto on March 9, and he would wait for Serra at Mission Santa María, the last in the mission chain, and just below Velicatá.

In the mountains which roll down the Gulf side of the peninsula, Serra left the regular northward trail and turning south followed a long sloping valley. Soon Mission San Francisco Javier de Biaundó came into view.

This mission is about twenty miles southwest from Loreto. It was the finest of the missions of Baja California, and has changed but little in the centuries since it was completed in 1759. The main portion of the church was built of dense volcanic stone instead of adobe, as in the case of so many of the old missions which have disappeared. The tower was built of lighter rock.

Serra remained at the mission three days because of his affection for Palóu and for supplies which he had been unable to get from the military at Loreto:

I tarried at the said mission for many reasons. One reason was the very particular affection I have had for many years for its minister, Father Professor Fray Francisco Palóu, my pupil. He was Commissary of the Holy Office, and appointed

by our college as my successor in the presidency of these missions, should I die or be absent for a considerable time. This last circumstance was the second motive for my staying; we had to deliberate about matters for which he would be responsible on my departure; to take measures for the well-being of these missions, what to get ready and prepare for the arrival at Loreto of the Most Illustrious Inspector who was expected shortly. The third reason, and for me the most worthy of remembrance, was to pay off in some measure my debt of gratitude.

Serra was referring to assistance given to him by Father Palóu in preparation for his long journey to the north:

The Reverend Father made up for what I lacked with such generous care—provisions in food, clothes for my own use, and traveling conveniences for the trip ahead of me—that I could not bring myself to count them all, nor leave them there, since, sinner that I am, I am still attached to what suits me well. May God reward so much generosity.

a prayer for strength

From the church and sacristy of San Javier Mission Serra chose articles which he could take for the new missions of Alta California. He chose, among other things, a silver chalice, a small bronze bell, a chausible of cloth of gold and a used red one.

At the altar of the mission Serra knelt in prayer before his departure. He would not heed the counsel of Palóu that he give up the journey and let Palóu go in his place:

Let us not speak of that. I have placed all my confidence in God, of whose goodness I hope that He will grant me to reach not only San Diego but also Monterey.

Palóu was disturbed and wrote to Gálvez about Serra's ailing leg and his insistence on going forward in spite of it. Gálvez replied:

I rejoice greatly that Reverend Father Junípero Serra is traveling along with the expedition. I praise the faith and the mighty confidence that he will recover and that God will permit him to arrive at San Diego. I also have the same confidence.

Dawn had barely come when Serra was lifted by two men onto the back of his mule. He turned to Palóu and said "Good-by, Francisco, until we meet in Monterey, where I hope we shall see each other and labor in the vineyard of the Lord." Palóu, as noted by Father Maynard Geiger, the biographer of Serra, was more voluble. He wrote years later of the farewell scene:

He said farewell, causing me equal pain for the love I felt for him and for the tenderness that I had owed him since the year 1740, when he began to be my teacher of philosophy. Since then we had almost always lived together, except when duty parted us, which was seldom and only for a short time. From this it may be inferred what reciprocal love there would be between teacher and pupil, and what sorrow that farewell would consequently cause us both, for we feared that we would not see each other again except in heaven.

Serra turned back along the trail over which he had come from Loreto, and soon afterward picked up the road that led northwest to the next mission, San José de Comondú, twelve leagues, or about thirty miles away.

at San José de Comondú

After leaving San Javier Serra had to cross a rather rough volcanic plain. At the edge of a deeply cut canyon in the *malpais* he could see the Mission of San José de Comondú.

To all travelers, from that day to this, it is always a thrilling sight in that rough, dry and hot country, to come suddenly upon this oasis of palms and agriculture.

The agriculture of today is probably very much as it was in the days of the mission. The mission had been a community for more than thirty years and vegetables were planted during fall and winter under deciduous fig trees which had lost their leaves. In summer crops would not grow in the shade under the cover of the leaves.

Serra arrived at the mission about eleven o'clock in the morning, after a ride of about thirty miles, and he was to remain for three more days. He found that its padre, Antonio Martínez, whom he had first met in Cadiz, Spain, on the way to the New World, and who later was a fellow missionary in the Sierra Gorda of Mexico, was not there:

The Father had gone to Mission La Purísima of which he was put in charge since the departure of its minister Father Preacher Fray Juan Crespí, who had set out with the first division of the expedition, as mentioned before. At any rate, thanks to the preparations made by the said Father Martínez in case I might arrive during his absence, I was short of nothing.

I sang the Mass and preached to the Indians of the mission or pueblo, who would have missed both had I not come; in this way and by hearing a certain number of confessions, my stay did not prove useless.

The next day there was an observance of another great feast day, the celebration of the Annunciation of Our Lady which had fallen on Holy Saturday. By Tuesday Father Martínez had arrived and helped Serra settle further details:

Meanwhile the mule drivers were fixing their loads and were at their wits' end for lack of blankets for the mules, ropes and hay, etc. All of which was soon set to rights by the generosity of the said Father, who insisted on my looking to see if anything else were wanting. May God reward him.

Father Serra now was back on the volcanic mesa following El Camino Real over which had passed the members of the first section of the land expedition, now on their way northward from Velicatá.

Leading from Comondú the road in sections appears today much as it did so long ago. It was built wide and the stones cleared to the side. Here is a section five miles from Comondú. The removal of protective stones and boulders which formed part of the desert pavement eventually exposed the road to slow erosion into a gully.

For over fifty years the Jesuit Fathers had walked along here in gradually extending their chain of missions northward. It has been used but little in the 200 years since Serra's time.

Also far ahead of him on the trail was the expedition's commander, Portolá, who was burdened with responsibilities that were facing him and with worries about Serra and his infected leg. He later described what had happened to him after leaving the presidio of Loreto:

While I was passing…through the missions established by the Jesuits to that one on the frontier named Santa María, we experienced no hardships worth mentioning, neither I nor my companions; for, in addition to the fact that we took from the presidio vegetables and delicacies, in exchange for the lamentations of the settlers, we were fortunate enough to be able to sleep under roofs, and make the march with some comfort.

In consideration of the great deserts into which I was going, and of the Russian hunger with which I foresaw we were going to contend, I was obliged to seize everything I saw as I passed through those poor missions, leaving them, to my keen regret, scantily provided for.

The instructions given to him by Gálvez had been detailed and firm:

I charge you with zeal and vigilance to maintain the most exact discipline of the soldiers of the expedition as well as over the muleteers, especially from the frontier on, so that the Indians will be well treated. The soldiers are to be punished as in the case of an irremissible crime if they offer any affront or violence to the women because besides being offenses against God, such excesses committed by them could also bring disaster to the entire expedition.

the water of life

Life on some parts of the Jesuit Trail was sustained by what the natives called *tinajas*. They are not springs but rocky catchments, or basins, which trap and hold rainfall and runoff water.

On the volcanic plain which Serra was crossing was a place called Tinaja Jesus del Monte. It has a catchment perhaps fifteen feet deep, and its water can last a year. Near here is a little chapel or way station dating from a period probably a little later than the time of the Sacred Expedition.

The missions themselves had been placed near sources of water, usually in the higher country of Baja California, and in the narrow valleys where brief seasonal flows occur.

While the countryside yielded water and food for those who were going by land, the sea was beginning to exact a toll. It was becoming only too clear why Gálvez had refused to allow Serra to go to Alta California by ship.

The *San Antonio* sailed in February and no log of her journey has ever been found. The *San Carlos*, sailing early in January, quickly ran into trouble. Within two weeks the crew had begun pumping water from her hold. On the second day of this it was discovered the water in the hold was fresh—the ship's caskets of drinking water had sprung leaks because of the constant pitching of the ship in heavy seas.

The *San Carlos* continued to run along the coast, and the appearance of the arid and sterile land frustrated hopes of obtaining a supply of fresh water.

On March 8 they sighted the grim and barren Cedros Island off Vizcaino Bay, halfway up the peninsula. The ship tacked back and forth, or lay becalmed, more than ten days, while land parties searched and finally found enough water to refill their fast-emptying casks.

Another ten days went by, as the *San Carlos* bucked adverse winds and squalls, or drifted in calms, before she finally was able to resume her northward tack. Twenty days had been lost. But heavy winds then blew her 200 miles off her course, and the scourge of the sea, scurvy, began to appear among the crew and passengers who were subsisting, as did most seamen of the time, on biscuits and salt or dried beef.

While the *San Carlos* and the *San Antonio* were wandering over an unfriendly sea, Father Serra came to the rim of the mesa and looked down upon the deep arroyo where stood Mission Purísima Concepción de Cadegomó.

Here the road wound a thousand feet down to the valley floor. Its seasonal river flowed west to the Pacific. It was noon when Serra reached the mission, which had been in the care of Father Crespí, after a ride of about twenty-five miles. He had been accompanied by Father Antonio Martínez, who had been with him in the Sierra Gorda, and since Crespí's assignment to the expedition, had been in charge of the mission at Comondú as well as at La Purísima.

Crespí had not forgotten his teacher and before leaving had taken pains to see that Serra would be provided for at least on this part of his journey. Serra related:

Before he left, he prepared different items for my equipment, and appointed the soldier Don Francisco María de Castro, Guard and Steward of this mission, to deliver them to me with whatsoever else might serve me. And so with such delicate attentions, the honors were paid us by this good soldier—Indian dances, too, and all the pomp and ceremony that is possible in such places...

Part of the preceding day was spent in putting in order the loads the mules had to carry, among which were four loads of biscuits, provided by order of the Captain and the forethought of Father Crespí, as provisions for the religious during the expedition, flour, ground corn, figs, raisins and whatever else might be of use to them. All that and what had been prepared by the Father in charge of San José Mission, as I mentioned, was put in order. My whole equipment and that of my companions was ready, and it was supplied much more abundantly than ever I could desire or imagine. Blessed be God!

From La Purísima a long journey lay ahead, over rugged country, before reaching Mission Nuestra Señora de Guadalupe. The trail they took went northwest and did not pass anywhere near Mission Santa Rosalía de Mulegé on the Gulf Coast which was a port of supply for the missions.

The trip now was constantly up the sierra, and when night approached, Serra stopped in open country at a place he identified as El Cardón. There is an El Cardón on the maps of Baja California today, but the location in Serra's time was somewhat farther east. Serra wrote:

I met there with about ten Indian families: men, women, boys and girls. When I asked them what they were doing there, they answered, with much sorrow, that they belonged to the Guadalupe Mission, not to any particular ranchería, but to the principal village, and that the Father, for lack of food, had been forced to send them to the mountains to look for food, and that, not being used to that way of life, they had had no success.

They suffered very much, especially at seeing their babies starve and hearing them cry. I pitied them very much, and though it was too bad the pack train was delayed and could not arrive that evening, they were not left without some relief, because from a supply of ground corn I had with me, a pot of good atole was made and distributed to the women and children; this was then repeated, the pot being filled a second time for the men. And so they were well satisfied. Still more so when I told them to return to their mission, that the Father had received corn by sea from the boat of Mulegé, as ordered by the Most Illustrious Inspector.

I went to rest, and they to pray in chorus; and they ended by singing a very touching hymn about the love of God. The Indians of that mission have quite a name for singing with especial sweetness, and so I found great consolation in listening to them.

In the morning, and still climbing, Serra's trail, clearly identifiable 200 years later, led down and up whatever ravines tended to run north and south instead of east and west. The Jesuits had taken advantage of this, as in the valley which lies south of Guadalupe Mission. In the days of the missions it was a cattle ranch and remnants of its stone works still exist.

After seventy-five miles of hard riding in two days, Serra arrived at Mission Nuestra Señora de Guadalupe, and took a much-needed rest. This was as far north as he had ever been in his short term as president of the missions of Baja California. From the doorway of Guadalupe Mission he could look out at the welcome shade of olive trees. Nothing today is left of the mission but a few mounds, but the orchard and water works are still clearly visible under the palms.

Serra's worn pack train came straggling in after him, and the mission Father, Juan Sancho, was anxious to render any help he could. Serra wrote:

Being told by my companions that among the animals impressed for the expedition the most miserable had been assigned to me, he ordered all the mules of his mission to be used in carrying the loads as far as the next mission. And that is what happened. It meant quite a relief, allowing my beasts to rest, and go without loads the next four days. And very necessary too since, even without loads, they were not all able to reach the next mission; one had to be abandoned half way, and another at the next mission.

The service rendered was all the greater when you consider that the few mules left in the mission, after the heavy requisition made by the Captain, were only the old and the decrepit: So much so that the Father, so much in need of food, as already mentioned, and knowing he certainly could get some at La Purísima, did not dare to send the mules for fear of finishing them off completely by that trip.

Father Sancho had one more favor to bestow, and one which Serra said was of more value to him than anything else:

He gave me, to wait upon me, a little page, his own till now, a smart Indian lad, fifteen years old, speaking Castilian and able to serve Mass, read and do any kind of service. He had him all fitted out with a change of clothes, leather jacket, boots, etc., and a horseman's complete outfit. He gave him a mule from his own saddle mules. The lad was thrilled; and were his parents proud of him!

Riding a fresh mule, Serra was making astonishing progress in spite of his sore leg. After leaving Guadalupe Mission the trail again led upward over the peninsular divide at an elevation of 4500 feet and east of the peak known as Cerro el Barranco.

Canyons were thick with garabatillo plants with their long wands covered with hooks which can scar the arms of unwary travelers.

At the divide he turned down a canyon into an area now known as San Sebastian and in some of the canyons he encountered ficus trees of immense size. Also here grew the legendary tree called a güéribo, which provided wood for the first boat ever built in Baja California, by Father Juan Ugarte in 1720.

Then it was up hill again, to a summit known as San Venancio. From here he could look down from one of the most spectacular viewpoints of his entire trip.

San Venancio marked the point where he would leave the plateau which he had been working along in the sierra for days. The trail led abruptly downward on the northern slope of the mountain for 2000 feet and came out on the high plain of San Ignacio.

The Jesuit trail, though heavily overgrown with brush, was clearly identified as late as 1968. It wound downward with thirteen or fourteen major switchbacks from one side of the canyon to the other. It had been carefully constructed with corners of the turns reinforced against washouts.

It was still rather early in the day when Serra rode down the meandering road, accompanied by his altar boy page, a soldier guard and other servants. His pack animals were a day ahead of him. The distance from Mission Guadalupe to the next mission was about thirty-five miles. But as the Jesuits had been splendid builders, the journey was made without incident and with little comment in the diaries by either Serra or Crespí.

the mists of Candelaria

The morning mist had barely lifted from the area known as Candelaria on the plain of San Ignacio. The sierra dropped away behind him as Serra traveled through volcanic country. Over a ridge lay a district identified by the missionaries as Santa Cruz.

He reached Santa Cruz, which is near the foot of the mountains, by midday, and after a rest, went on to the rancheria of San Borja, where he would spend the night in the open. The maps of later generations identify the place as San Borjita.

Far to the north, and unknown to Serra, as well as to Portolá and Crespí, the supply ship *San Antonio* had completed a successful voyage.

She had not encountered the same difficulties as the *San Carlos* but missed the Port of San Diego. Vizcaíno had described the port as the best in all the South Sea but had placed it in the wrong latitude, and the *San Antonio* had wandered among the Channel Islands for some time. At one of the islands the crew took on water, and when the heathen Indians found and returned a lost staff with its iron cross,

the grateful crew named the island Santa Cruz, or Holy Cross.

Convinced they were too far north, the crew turned back and on April 11 found and entered the Bay of San Diego. The entrance to the port is at 32 degrees and 40 minutes north latitude. Vizcaíno's log had placed it at 33 degrees and 30 minutes or near San Pedro Bay. The *San Antonio* had been at sea fifty-five days.

Meanwhile, the *San Carlos* was still bucking adverse winds and for a month had been unable to get farther north than about the 28th parallel, or just about the vicinity of Cedros Island. A tragedy was beginning to unfold.

The ship's log recorded the first death at one o'clock in the afternoon of April 18 or 19. It was that of a boatswain's second mate. Several days later, the log again took up the count:

On this day the sick and those who had not yet fulfilled their religious duties confessed and received the sacrament. At one o'clock in the evening, the pilot, Manuel Reyes, died...at eight o'clock in the morning, the body of Reyes was cast overboard.

El Camino Real held no terrors for Serra, and there often was the unexpected thoughtfulness of his fellow missionaries.

The road he was following toward San Ignacio, while up and down, as usual, was made for swift traveling. At Santa Cruz, it followed ridges and narrow canyons and even 200 years later could be easily located. Stones had been collected from the trail and piled along the edges to form a definite border.

Soon after he had stopped for the night in open Indian country, a group of Indians appeared — but they were Christianized Indians and they brought with them a prepared supper that had been sent out by Father Juan León de Medina Veitía at the mission of San Ignacio.

Resuming his journey in the morning, Serra soon overtook the mule drivers who had preceded him. Again Serra took pains to comment on the equipment and supplies that had been given to him and his people by the military, this time re-telling a story related to him by the mule drivers:

Their news was all about their attempting to shoot with a very second-rate gun issued from the Loreto office to Carlos Rubio, one of the two new soldiers who came with me, without the Commissary Trillo's allowing him to exchange it for another, as was requested. When he tried to fire it, the barrel burst from top to bottom and burned the whole hand of the soldier, Marcelo Bravo, who discharged it. For days the wounded man could not help with the pack train. So I left with them, to take his place, one of the boys who came with me; and I continued my trip.

Not long afterward he met Father Medina Veitía who had come a league's distance to welcome him. After greetings had been exchanged, and the news of the day discussed, Medina went on ahead to return to his mission, where he donned a surplice, stole and cope, and surrounded himself with his Christian Indians to formally await the arrival of the Father President at about nine o'clock in the morning.

Serra's journey to the missionary frontier was not yet half over.

After a long and hot ride over cactus-studded volcanic country the date palms of San Ignacio gave promise of rest and coolness. The palms had been planted by the Jesuit fathers in an arroyo rich with several springs. Serra stayed at the original Jesuit adobe church though a new stone structure was being erected nearby.

Relatively pleasant in summer and winter, San Ignacio is situated at an elevation of about 500 feet, and Serra easily bowed to Father Medina's entreaties that he remain for another day:

Sunday, the day of the profession of our Father Saint Francis, and also the day our order celebrates the feast of Saint Raphael, the Archangel, patron of travelers. I observed the day by resting, and made the renewal of my own profession, as do all our religious in the whole world today. While I intended to start the following day, the said Reverend Father besought me to delay at least one more day, for many reasons he brought forward. I felt bound to grant his humble request.

During his stay here Serra commented on the troubles of Father Medina while assigned to Mission Santa María de Los Angeles. Medina had been distressed, or as Serra wrote, "his mind was never at rest," owing to the inability to raise enough food to care for the native Indians who had gathered at the mission and accepted baptism. San Ignacio, with all its agricultural richness, had witnessed a drastic decline of the Indians who had not been able to adjust to changes in their way of life, or resist diseases brought by Europeans.

Serra and his fellow missionaries recruited from the missions all they would need to conduct services in a pagan land. At San Ignacio Serra obtained a silver chalice with its paten and spoon, a censer with its silver boat, a silver shell for baptizing, a pair of silver cruets with their plate and a silver bell, a white satin cloth with trimming and fringe of gold, a white vestment of Persian silk with silver flowers, four small metal candlesticks and six bronze candlesticks, three small Sanctus bells of metal, a consecrated altar stone, and some altar cloths.

In a letter to his successor, Father Palóu, he mentioned that he had been carrying out the orders of Gálvez, the Inspector General:

The memorandum which His Most Illustrious Lordship prepared concerning that which could be drawn from the missions had been carried out superabundantly.

entering El Infierno

In the morning I left San Ignacio. Not having started early, and the day being very warm, I was unable to make the regular day's march. I stopped at noon in scorching heat, taking refuge in a cave, called, I was told, La Magdalena.

Upon leaving the mission Serra had headed directly toward another range of mountains, and to the east he could see three volcanic peaks known as the Tres Virgenes, or the Three Virgins. They are just north of Santa Rosalía.

Spring was arriving, but climatically in that section of Baja California it was already summer.

Serra's trail led almost across the mountains to the eastern slopes and into the mouth of a canyon know as El Infierno, or The Inferno. Even as today, the entrance to the canyon had many beautiful palo blanco trees with their white bark which contrasted with red buttes which were hot to the touch.

Most of the Jesuit road through Baja California had been well built and maintained in excellent condition, and was trod regularly by couriers going from one mission to another. But once inside a place like El Infierno, even the Jesuits couldn't build a road and Serra had to scramble over the rocks as best he could.

When the simmering heat had begun to fade, Serra resumed his ride but had to spend the night in the open fields again. It was a long way to his next stop, as Mission Santa Gertrudis was about fifty-five miles north of San Ignacio over rough country.

At Santa Gertrudis, Serra knew that he would face a difficult situation. The country was not a happy one and Gálvez had suggested that most of the families trying to exist in the mission village be removed to Purísima Mission. Serra later wrote:

There they will be assured of good meals three times a day and suitable clothing, all of which they never had nor will ever find in their present mission, or perhaps I had better say, mountains. There they have no land for cultivation, nor any possibility of it.

In the end they refused to leave their homeland.

the trail to Santa Marta

Emerging from El Infierno, Serra, as well as Crespí before him, had looked down upon the plain of Santa Marta. It might have seemed that travel would be easier. But the plain was a gigantic rock pile.

Also here the old Jesuit road has no paralleling trail to this day, and infrequent settlers ride the same path as did the Fathers so long ago.

For two days and a part of a third Serra continued on the trail, sleeping in the open. At Mission Santa Gertrudis he was welcomed with Indian dances and received the sprinkling of holy water from Father Dionisio Basterra. Serra wrote:

For many days the Father had fallen into a deep melancholy from loneliness, hemmed in by so many Indians, without soldiers or servants—the Captain (Rivera) had taken both away for his expedition—and without an interpreter worth the name.

Basterra told how he pleaded with Portolá for soldiers for protection:

He treated the Governor with all possible courtesy; but the reply was that, not only could he not give him an escort, but that he made up his mind to take it away from the next mission, San Borja, which had always at least three soldiers.

Serra was sorry for the minister who had shared with him experiences in Mexico:

So all of this—together with my tender love for this young religious, ever since the time he trained for the apostolic ministry of missions among the faithful, being my companion as we evangelized all along the coast of Oaxaca, as we sailed up the river Los Miges, and preached in the city of Antequera, and also on our return journey along the King's highway back to Mexico—all of this explains how we gave vent to that sudden storm of tears, being so happy to see each other again after a little more than a year from our arrival in California, and our last parting at Loreto.

The northern frontier was not far ahead. For two and a half days Serra and the soldiers rode up the spine of the San Borja Mountains, in the manner indicated in this old sketch of freight transportation in Baja California, with their water in leather bags and barrels tied to mules. Then they began their descent to the high desert of Santa María. The same trip had taken Crespí and his fifteen Indian escorts three and a half days.

Both of them evidently avoided the arroyo of El Paraiso, about 1200 feet deep, which slashes through the mountains in an east-west direction and which was mentioned by every north-south traveler for more than a century with the exception of members of the Sacred Expedition.

The old Jesuit trail now sees only an occasional cowboy going from one ranch to another. Along the trail is a stone with a carved cross, balanced upon a large rock. How long it has helped weary travelers safely on their way is not known.

In a few days Serra would leave the land of the missionaries, and would find death a companion, though not to the degree of the men of the sea.

Far to the north, the *San Carlos,* at last sailing clear, sighted the islands that Vizcaíno had called Los Coronados, and Captain Vila noted in the ship's log:

They are the best and surest marks for making the Port of San Diego which is situated about five and a half leagues due north of these islands.

It was April 28, and she had been at sea for 110 days. Because of a thick bed of kelp and because of a lack of wind, the *San Carlos* was unable to penetrate into the harbor itself, until late the following day, and then Captain Vila signaled to the *San Antonio* which was anchored at Point Guijarros, now known as Ballast Point:

We broke out our colors. She broke out hers...at eight o'clock at night a launch of the San Antonio *came with her second in command and pilot, Don Miguel del Pino, who gave us an account of her voyage. She arrived...with half of her crew down with scurvy, of which two men had died. They had only the seven men who came in the launch fit for work...Captain Juan Pérez was also in poor health, and only the two missionaries were well.*

33

Thirteen years before Serra passed through this country the Jesuits had begun building a chapel at San Borja. The approach to San Borja was over the plain of El Gentil. To Serra the land was even drier than the Baja California he had known. The mountains were dropping away and the true desert was taking over.

The Jesuits expected that a mission at San Borja would become an important link in a mission chain they had hoped to string around the upper end of the Gulf of California to connect with their missions on the mainland in Sonora.

The Mission San Francisco de Borja was put into the service of the Indians a few years later by Father Link, whose reports of unexplored country to the north would be followed by the Portola-Serra expedition.

The land was too poor to provide enough food for the hundreds of Indians in the area who tried in vain to change from a hunting to an agricultural people. The Jesuit era had run out and now the Franciscans were responsible for the welfare of the Indians.

When Serra arrived he said the mission was in the care of Father Fermín Francisco de Lasuén, who in the years ahead would succeed Serra as president of the missions of Alta California:

We passed the day in discussing matters pertaining to the expedition and the pagan country—he was very anxious to join us—in visiting the building of the poor mission with its teeming numbers, and in speaking about the next one where the Father had been for some considerable time during the absence of its own minister.

Lasuén replaced the original Jesuit chapel with another adobe church, and it in turn was replaced by one erected of stone by the Dominicans who eventually succeeded the Franciscans in Baja California.

Four days of travel over open, dusty desert stretched out from San Borja, for both Serra and Crespí ahead of him.

Twelve leagues, or about thirty miles beyond the mission, Crespí reached another of Baja California's life-saving water catchments, which was identified as the Tinaja de Jubay. Here a rock formation, appearing as a cave with a darkened opening, trapped water and stored it the year around, safe from evaporation.

This is the most famous catchment in Baja California, and without it north-south travel in this region would have been impossible. It would have been a four-day run without water for mules. Crespí drank, and slept in the open in the cold of the desert night.

Six weeks behind Crespí came Serra. He, too, found rest after a tiring day's journey, at Jubay:

From my previous stopping place, I arrived at that of Jubay, and remained there because I felt tired, although there was plenty of time to push on in the afternoon.

Crespí has told how he left the watering place and resumed his ride toward the next mission:

March 18, I set out from this place early in the morning, and about two or three leagues past Jubay, a mule carrying provisions gave out, and remained stretched out in the road, unable to go further. The soldier accompanying me had to stay behind with some Indians to see whether they could bring it on after resting, and I went on to reach the old mission of Santa María, called Calamajué. I pressed forward with my own two Indian youths and some other Indians from the missions who were following me.

I went the whole day at a good pace, stopping only a little while at noon, to eat a bite, and about ten o'clock at night came to the mission at Calamajué, where I found a messenger from Santa María from the Reverend Father Fray Fermín Lasuén, with vestments and everything else needed that I had asked for from back at his Mission San Borja to be able to say Mass at this place, the next day, Palm Sunday.

On my arrival, as it was so late at night, I told them to make me some chocolate, and then retired to rest, for I was indeed worn out.

a country of sadness

The bleakness of the country left both Serra and Crespí rather sad. Both of them stopped for a night's rest at a place called Calamajué, where the Jesuits had abandoned their effort to establish a mission. They had been defeated by a land heavy with salt. The available water was unpalatable. Crespí wrote of what he did at the deserted church:

March 19th dawned, Palm Sunday and St. Joseph's day: I said my Matins and Prime in no great hurry. The sun was rising when I had them arrange the Altar in the Church that still existed on this spot. Meanwhile I waited for the soldier to come with the pack mule that gave out yesterday, as I had promised to wait the Mass for him. I went on to pray the minor hours, and then spent some time walking around in the vicinity of this place, passing the time.

Since I had arrived at night, I had not seen what it was like, and I was amazed to find everything so bare, high hills and everything else, with nothing in sight but rocks and bare ground, and if this is not good mining country, then I do not know what to say, for there is not a bush in sight

…In this way it got near eleven o'clock, and still no sign of my soldier. I warned the Indians to be ready and went to say Mass, since it was a long one for Passion Sunday, and needed the time.

At four in the afternoon the soldier arrived with the pack mule carrying my effects. I had wanted to go on today after the Mass, to join the main body of the expedition as soon as possible, for I know that Captain Rivera, commanding, is to set out shortly, but what happened has forced me to remain here today; will get up early tomorrow, please God.

Serra, traveling over a "most tortuous" road known as El Caxón, reached Calamajué on May 3. The next day he observed the Feast of the Ascension, and a notation in his diary suggests that mail service was being maintained regularly between the missions and divisions of the Sacred Expedition:

I said Mass in that deserted church, a shack, all in ruins, and the rest of the morning I answered all the letters which required replies. The mail went by a little after midday for the mission of San Borja.

the last of the missions

The Jesuits had built no farther north than Mission Santa María de los Ángeles, and in his diary Crespí reported for himself and Serra how the missionary outpost appeared. It was situated a mile up a rocky arroyo that 200 years later was impassable for animals. A rock slide at the entrance had choked the canyon:

This Mission Santa María de los Angeles lies to the northwest on the borders of heathendom. Since it has been such a short time established it is as yet quite poor. It is situated on a creek between very high, rugged hills that here makes a small valley, with many tall palm trees round about. There are a good many waterholes throughout the vicinity with very fine delicious waters.

Though I, for the short time I spent there, was unable to make an examination and instruct myself of everything, yet the Reverend Father President, reaching here in the second section of the expedition with the Governor, had leisure to examine all the nearby waterholes of the area, and found everything much to his taste.

There are tracts with grass and water for cattle, and by turning water from the springs onto certain slopes offering possibilities of irrigation, a cultivation might be achieved, little if at all inferior to that of the former missions. Wherefore, his Reverence, having previously been informed of the miserable state of this mission, and very much inclined to its abandonment or extinction, having seen it, wrote most earnestly and most forcefully to his Most Illustrious Lordship the Visitor General, to have it preserved.

It was here that Serra at last caught up with his expedition's commander, Captain Portolá. All of the complaints of the past were forgotten:

There I met the Governor with the Father Fray Miguel de la Campa. A part of the company already had gone ahead to Velicatá, for there was plenty of grass there, and it was entirely lacking here. We were as happy as possible to see each other, all eager to start on our new venture across the desert land, for a country peopled by pagans in great numbers.

San Luis Gonzaga Bay

From a ship in the Bay of San Luis Gonzaga on the Gulf Coast, the Portolá and Serra section of the Sacred Expedition received its last supplies. Four days were required to move the supplies by pack train along the twenty-five mile trail from the bay to the mission.

Above Santa María at Velicatá Captain Rivera had left perhaps several hundred head of cattle, and almost 200 horses and mules, to fatten on pasturage and to be taken to Alta California at a later date.

Instead of two days, as had been planned, Rivera and Father Crespí were now ranging far ahead of Portolá and Serra. Rivera believed in traveling light and had taken only enough food for two meals a day.

In a letter to Father Palóu, Crespí wrote of his feelings about the Captain:

Words fail me in which to tell your Reverence of the dangers that this man put us in because of his whims.

Crespí's diary tells us about their start from Velicatá:

This first section of the expedition...is made up of...twenty-five leather-jacketed soldiers, Don José Cañizares, three muleteers, and about forty-two Christian Indians from our fartherest missions...Many of them did not get even as far as Santa María, but ran away, and some of those who did reach here, reached here ill; I am sorry for it and wonder how these poor souls will stand the journey ahead.

Serra lingered at Santa María, which at that time even lacked a resident minister, and though he did not mention it, his leg was beginning to give him serious trouble. The time came to leave:

I took my leave of these poor Indians, distressed at leaving them for the time being, without a minister, hoping however that such a sad condition would not last very long.

In his usual matter-of-fact manner, Portolá described how they took to the trail for the three-day ride to Velicatá:

I set out from Santa María, the last mission to the north, escorted by four soldiers, in company with Father Junípero Serra, president of the missions, and Father Miguel Campa.

CHAPTER II *The Frontier*

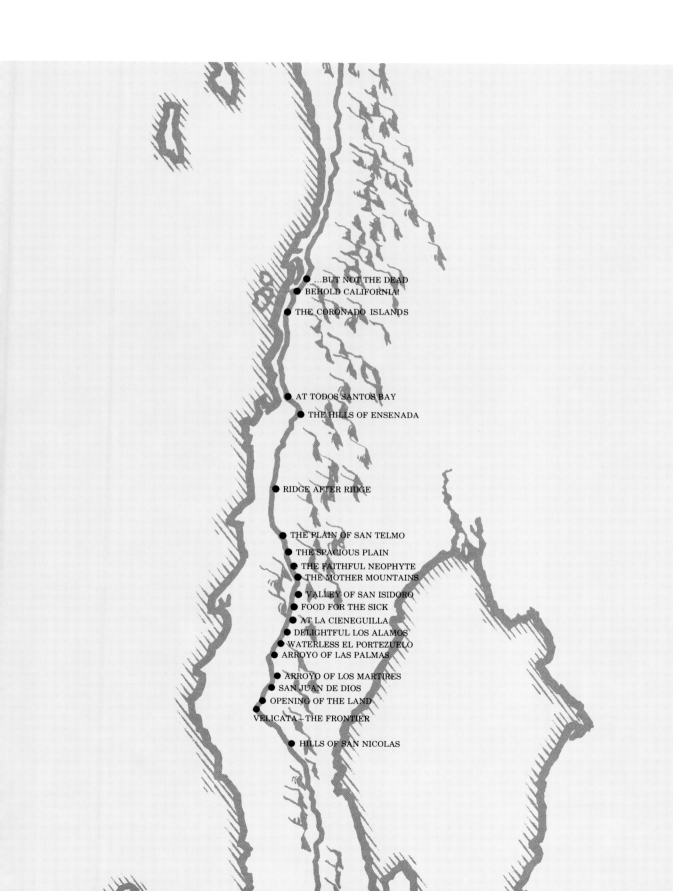

- ...BUT NOT THE DEAD
- BEHOLD CALIFORNIA!
- THE CORONADO ISLANDS
- AT TODOS SANTOS BAY
- THE HILLS OF ENSENADA
- RIDGE AFTER RIDGE
- THE PLAIN OF SAN TELMO
- THE SPACIOUS PLAIN
- THE FAITHFUL NEOPHYTE
- THE MOTHER MOUNTAINS
- VALLEY OF SAN ISIDORO
- FOOD FOR THE SICK
- AT LA CIENEGUILLA
- DELIGHTFUL LOS ALAMOS
- WATERLESS EL PORTEZUELO
- ARROYO OF LAS PALMAS
- ARROYO OF LOS MARTIRES
- SAN JUAN DE DIOS
- OPENING OF THE LAND
- VELICATA – THE FRONTIER
- HILLS OF SAN NICOLAS

hills of San Nicolás

The journey of forty miles to Velicatá excited Serra. This was virgin territory and most certainly populated with pagans who had not yet experienced the blessings of Christianity.

He and Portolá along with Father Campa set out with only four soldiers for protection. The route was over rough hills and at the evening of the first day they came to a place called San Nicolás. Along their route late in the day they could look westward across the hills etched against an evening sun:

Bright and early we set out—the two Fathers with the Governor—and pretty soon we ran across the little river I mentioned and followed it for more than a league. It was a sight to see—palm trees, grass and water in abundance, and stretches of land suitable for irrigation, orchards and grain. It promised well for the mission. The water could be dammed at a sufficient altitude. And so there seemed to be nothing to stand in the way of permanent improvement. Leaving the river.bank, we pushed on our way halting at noon by the

San Antonio River. In the afternoon we made a little less than two leagues, reaching a place called San Nicolás.

The next two days they saw footprints of Indians and their huts, but the Indians fled on the approach of White men:

We arrived at the place called Sweet Water. On the way we saw various little rancherías of pagan Indians and recent footprints; but none of them neither young nor old, did we see; and so I had to give up any thought of speaking to them and winning their good graces...after traveling the whole day, we arrived at evening at Velicatá, where all the soldiers that were there gave us a great reception.

Again we saw some little huts of Indians, and their footprints, but nothing of them. All that stretch of country needs still more help than the rest of California, owing to the poverty of its inhabitants. As a matter of fact, from Santa María as far as here, I did not see a single pitahaias tree, whether sweet or sour; nothing but, here and there, the cardón, garabatillo and cirio, a tree completely useless, even for burning.

Velicatá—the frontier

At Velicatá, Serra established the first mission to be founded by Franciscans in Baja California. It was the time of the Pentecost. A crude hut left by the first division of the Sacred Expedition was cleaned out and prepared for a religious observance:

In the hut, then, they prepared the altar, the soldiers putting on their full accoutrements, leather jackets and shields, and with all the surroundings of Holy poverty, I celebrated the Mass on that great day, so consoled with the thought that it was the first of many to be continued permanently in this new mission of San Fernando, thus founded that very day.

While the celebration lasted, repeated discharges of firearms by the soldiers added to the solemnity; and for once the smoke of powder took the place of burning incense, which we could not use because we had none with us...The congregation was made up of ourselves, the soldiers and the Indian neophytes who came with us, while no gentiles dared come near, frightened perhaps by so much shooting.

The next day the pack train arrived, and with it came candles for the celebration of Mass:

It was a great day of joy because just after the Mass...they came to tell me that Indians were coming and were close by. I gave praise to the Lord, kissing the ground, and thanking His Majesty...He now permitted me to be among the pagans in their own country...I saw something I could not believe when I had read of it, or had been told about it. It was this: they were entirely naked, as Adam in the garden, before sin. So they go, and so they presented themselves to us. We spoke a long time with them, and not for one moment, while they saw us clothed, could you notice the least sign of shame in them for their own lack of dress.

Father Campa was left in charge to see to the building of a mission. The Indian who posed as captain was advised that while in the past his authority had come from the wish and whim of his people, he now "ruled in the name of our Lord the King."

The border of the frontier dropped away behind Serra and Portolá as they turned northward once again up the backbone of Baja California. They had come more than 400 miles from Loreto. San Diego was almost 300 miles beyond Velicatá.

The first section of the land expedition, led by Rivera and Crespí, included about thirty-one White men and somewhere between forty-four and fifty-two Baja California Indian auxiliaries. The second section, with Portolá and Serra, included sixteen Whites and about forty-four Indians. Thus on the trail was a long and scattered train numbering perhaps as many as 130 persons. Most, if not all of the Whites were mounted. The Indians walked. The two pack trains must have had at least several hundred mules and horses.

Crespí and Rivera opened the way beyond Velicatá and after two hours' of travel they halted in a dry arroyo in the blazing colors of a desert sunset. The next morning, the march was resumed. Crespí wrote:

After about a league and a half of travel we came out from among the hills and entered the open country with good-sized plains, but the barrenness of the land and the scarcity of water continued, with the difference that we now found some grass in some places.

Neither Portolá or Serra, at the time, dwelt on their thoughts as the tiring march into new territory began. A number of years later, however, Portolá had the occasion to recall his thoughts and have them set down:

I began my march to the bay named San Diego, in company with thirty soldiers of the presidio and many Indian auxiliaries; but, in a few days we saw with extreme regret that our food was gone, with no source of supplies unless we should turn back. As a result, some of the Indians died, and the rest of them deserted from natural necessity. So I was left alone with the cuirassiers; without stopping the march, we went on, lamenting, now to the mountains to kill geese and rabbits, now to the beach for clams and small fish, and then in search of water, which we did not find for three or four days, the animals going twice that long without drinking, as we ourselves did sometimes.

San Juan de Diós

On the third day out of Velicatá Serra acknowledged his lameness. This was at a place they called San Juan de Diós, "an agreeable spot with abundant water, pasture, willows, tules and a smiling sky." Here near the base of one of the landmark peaks of the region, the expedition waited for stragglers. Serra wrote:

I said Mass there, but I had much trouble in standing on my feet, because the left one was much inflamed. For a year now the swelling has reached halfway up my leg, which is covered with sores. That is why for the rest of the time we stayed here, I had to lie prostrate most of the time upon my bed, and I was afraid that before long I should have to follow the expedition on a stretcher.

Meanwhile they were busying themselves, the Governor and his men, in preparing the pack loads, dividing the sections of the train, and getting into condition the animals that had arrived last and needed to recuperate.

Despite his ailment, Serra was overjoyed upon receiving a letter from Velicatá in which Father de la Campa said that an Indian captain who Serra had befriended had returned to the mission with eleven companions and all wanted to receive Holy Baptism.

At San Juan de Diós, Portolá, concerned over Serra's condition, tried to convince him to return to Velicatá and to recuperate at leisure. Serra refused:

Your Honor, please do not speak of that, for I trust that God will give me the strength to reach San Diego, as He has given me the strength to come so far. In case He does not, I will conform myself to His most Holy will. Even though I should die on the way, I shall not turn back. They can bury me wherever they wish and I shall gladly be left among the pagans, if it be the will of God.

Instead, Serra induced a muleteer to prepare the same remedy that he would administer to an animal, tallow mixed with some green herbs from the field, and had it applied to his leg as a poultice. In the morning, much improved, he celebrated Mass, and resumed the journey.

arroyo of Los Mártires

The trail described by the Jesuit explorer Father Link was now their road toward the northwest. The diary of José Cañizares, who kept the record of the march for Rivera, tells for the first time the suffering of the Indians who had left their ancient homelands to accompany the expedition:

In the morning Holy Mass was said, and about eight o'clock we were told that a Christian Indian was very sick. The Father went to see him, and, at the same time, to try to confess him. Being unsuccessful in this he absolved him, and under these circumstances the Indian died at eleven o'clock. Because of this occurrence and the fact that we found sufficient pasturage to refresh the animals, we decided not to leave until three o'clock in the afternoon.

Starting at that time we traveled over a route to the northwest by west, and then we swung to the west-northwest. Having advanced about three leagues over level country, we arrived at half past six at an arroyo called Los Mártires, where we found pools of water and abundant pasturage...The Captain posted his men to watch the camp and the animals, and *nothing in the least eventful happened.*

The next day they followed the course of the arroyo of Los Mártires which runs toward the west coast of the peninsula. In the distance to the northeast they could see Cerro Matomi. Twice they were halted by rain. Crespí noted that the Captain permitted him to "put the poor shelter which I carry inside his good-sized tent." Two other Indians became seriously ill and Crespí attended them and administered the Holy Extreme Unction.

Along the same trail, which here enters the southern foothills of Sierra de San Pedro Martir, Serra and his party saw a group of Indians on a hill. A neophyte was sent to invite them to come down and accept their friendship, but they fled.

They did find one old man, naked as the rest, who recalled that another Father, who must have been a Jesuit priest, had been through the region, and though the rest of his tribe had fled, he had stood his ground. He said he was willing to become a Christian, and Serra arranged that he be sent to Velicatá for instruction.

arroyo of Las Palmas

Along the trail the missionaries kept a lookout for sites for additional missions the Franciscans might want to establish on the route to Alta California.

They were finding the country opening up, but the land was sterile, without pasture and without any trees other than the spiny cirios and cacti of Baja California, and here and there a low valley with some palms.

They actually were following a route that never was to be used again, and from the diaries it is difficult to trace their steps very accurately. The Jesuits never went over this ground except for Father Link on two reconnoitering expeditions. So no trail was ever built.

The number of sick Indian auxiliaries was increasing. During a day's march one of the two ailing Indians with Rivera and Crespí died. Crespí wrote:

He belonged to the mission of San Ignacio...I buried him before we set out, at the spot where I said Mass yesterday, and a cross was left set up over his grave. It is ordered that the other Indian...shall be carried on a hurdle, and the Commander has ordered that the five who are not so ill shall return to their missions, with two or three of the well ones to accompany them.

They camped that night in an arroyo on the northern branch of Río del Rosario which they called Las Palmas. Some of the palm trees there were very large, but there was no spring nor running water. They obtained water by digging a well. Serra later in his diary named the area Santiago.

The word "road" appears in all the diaries and the assumption is that they generally followed Indian trails, whenever possible. Serra said that before they reached some open country they had found the "road" very difficult:

We continued our journey, leaving the river and taking to the hills in the direction of the west coast...the road was all steep hills, rocky and tiresome, up hill and down dale, till we came to some level mesas where we found evident signs that the first division of the expedition had stopped there. We did likewise. As there was no water in sight, we dug a water hole for the animals to drink. However, a little later we saw we might have saved ourselves the trouble, as a league or so farther on, running water was found, and good pasture.

The forbidding land was not welcoming strangers. For both sections of the expedition scouts ranged ahead to open the way and search for camp sites with water.

Crespí said that they entered another dry arroyo which had a palm or two, and then descended through a small pass with the country opening out wide, with some palms and surrounded by hills, through which they came to another dry arroyo which he named San Angelo de Fulgino:

At it we pitched camp. We had brought water in two barrels and in the leather bags for the use of the men had we found none; there was none for the horses, but they had drunk their fill at noon, before we set out.

This was in a region just west of a mountain and a settlement identified on today's maps as El Portezuelo.

Serra and his party had the same experience and their animals had to go without water. The next day's march was under a blazing sun which he said made the journey very painful, and at night rest did not always come easily:

For the last four nights a roaring lion quite close by kept us awake. May God guard us from it, as He has until now. On the way some cottontails were seen; only two were caught. Also there were footprints of gentiles but not one was seen.

The diary of Cañizares throws some more light on the Indians in this particular country through which the expedition passed:

At five o'clock in the morning we were told that one of the two Indians who had received the Extreme Unction yesterday had died and that three more had fallen ill. This aroused the Captain's suspicion, so he ordered all the Indians to assemble, urging them to continue on such a Holy expedition as ours, and not to assume that those who had died had done so as a result of joining our enterprise.

Later he reported an incident that indicated the Christianized, or neophyte, Indians were caught between fires:

Three of the sick Indians whom we had left in the arroyo of Los Mártires arrived in camp. They said that after we had left, ten heathen had descended upon them, and their fear of these heathen had caused them to return to us. The other two had gone on to Velicatá.

delightful Los Alamos

About eight days out of Velicatá the country began to change from arid to semi-arid. The trail-breakers saw their first trees and the spirits of the expedition began to lift. At the arroyo of Los Alamos they camped at a place named by Father Link. The youthful and enthusiastic Cañizares wrote:

The appearance of this arroyo of Los Alamos is beautiful. Because of the trees which clothe its banks, and the presence of rabbits and goats, deer, and brightly colored birds, it is a delightful spot for a house.

Crespí and Serra were more matter-of-fact about the place, but both noted the presence of trees and many flowers and that running water and pasture were found a little farther down the road. Here Serra and Portolá rested.

They sighted two Indians on a hill and soldiers were sent out to stalk them. One slipped through their hands. Serra tells us:

The other they tied with ropes, and it was as well they did, for even so he still fought against them, flinging himself to

the ground with such violence as badly to injure legs and knees. But finally they succeeded in bringing him in, and setting him on his knees before me. I placed my hands on his head and recited the Gospel of Saint John, blessed him with the sign of the Cross and had him set free.*

The Indian was given figs, meat and tortillas to eat, and then excused himself for having spied upon the expedition, for the purpose of ambushing and killing its members. As Serra wrote:

What he wished to do was understandable enough. But in explaining this venial sin he was betrayed into admitting a mortal sin, when he told us that he had been sent by his chiefs and their rancherías — and they were all assembled for the attack — lying in ambush behind the rocks, should surprise the Father and all accompanying him, and put them to death no matter how numerous they might be.

We pardoned him his murderous intentions, and loading him down with presents we let him go in order that he might tell his people how well we treated him.

San Isidoro, a fourth of the way on the long road to San Diego, was the most pleasant place the expedition encountered after leaving Velicatá. Serra and Portolá were greeted by Indians who went leaping up and down, running and shouting, and going from one side of the road to the other with joyful expressions.

When Rivera and Crespí had passed through the country, however, there had been a pause to bury another Indian auxiliary from Santa Gertrudis Mission, who had died on the trail.

This inviting valley runs from northwest to southeast and two small rivers, which rise in the Sierra San Pedro Martir, branch out from the two sides of the valley and join somewhere in the middle. Crespí bestowed on the valley the name of San Isidoro because his party stopped there on that saint's day. However, Portolá gave the valley another name, and for the same reason, that he and Serra arrived on the day of still another saint, as recorded by Serra:

We rested today, the Feast of our Patron San Fernando, King of Spain. In a palm-branch shelter that the soldiers had got ready the day before, hung around with blankets, and tastefully decorated, I said Mass with much happiness of heart. This place, declares the Governor, should be called San Fernando, not only because we arrived here on the evening before the Saint's day, and Mass was celebrated on his feast, but more particularly because it is the king of sites in California.

There is no mission, of all I have seen, which, even after all improvements have been made, can present so fair a view as this spot; and all its attractions have been given it by the Lord, the Author of Nature… The leafy greenage of the place forms a semicircle with a rock-ribbed hill in the middle, on which the mission or village could be established; and from here, without any fear of dampness, a wonderful view of this paradise of beauty could be enjoyed.

Should it be that the mission at Velicatá keeps the name of San Fernando, distinct from Santa María, I would be delighted if this should be called San Pedro Regalado; but, for the present, I will name this place by the saint of the day, San Fernando. May Our Lord God grant us soon to see this spot settled.

Higher and higher ridges rose before them when the sections of the expedition skirted the green and blue foothills of the San Pedro Martir Mountains. For the first time both sections of the expedition noted the presence of a number of streams which were in fact at that season flowing rivers. At the first one, Crespí recalled:

This little river has a considerable width and amount of water, running in a deeply sunken bed so overgrown with cottonwoods, willows and other trees, in the middle as well as on the banks, that when we were faced with having to get across it (and cross it indeed we did as many as nine times), it was necessary to cut down trees in some places. This river flows very much sunken in, with no good soil on any side, only extremely high hills, and in order to get by it one is forced to zig-zag along the few slopes offered by their sides.

His party struggled through the foothills, riding and resting, for three days:

All the hills and knolls of this day's march (are) clothed with what they call Romerillos, very fragrant, many bushes like the juniper in their leaf, small-sized oaks, some dwarf pines, and other shrubs not known to us.

Romerillos referred to sagebrush.

Portolá and Serra were in the same region for four days and Serra says that as they approached the "immense wall of high mountains" they had to turn in a southerly direction, as there was no other way to proceed, and then turned west. He saw a country green and rich:

It seems the rocks and thorns of California have disappeared...there are flowers in abundance and beautiful ones...and that nothing should be wanting in that direction, when we came to our stopping place, we met the queen of flowers—the Rose of Castile...blessed be He who created them.

The Rose of Castile is a small wild pink rose that reminded all of the early explorers of Spain. Serra says they camped by a river thick with roses as well as wild grapes:

We stayed in this place so that the animals might take advantage of the fine pasture and the water of the River of Roses. So it may be named because, after having examined it more at my leisure today, I saw so many rose bushes in flower that a purveyor of perfume could easily make a fortune.

PORTRAIT OF A NATIVE INDIAN

Though the richness of the land, in comparison to the deserts over which they had come, lifted their spirits, sickness and death cast conflicting shadows. Crespí recalls while struggling through the rough foothills of the mountains:

I said Mass early in the morning in order to give the viaticum to a soldier named Guillermo Carrillo, whom they have been carrying on a hurdle since the Cieneguilla; to whom I also administered the Holy oils, as he is very ill with the pleurisy.

Though the country was good the Indians were poor. At one of their camping places, the Indian neophytes who were following the expedition on foot brought in a heathen Indian with three girls and a baby boy, all much exhausted, and as Crespí wrote:

They were all of them painted in stripes.

The girls…were decently covered with a thick bunch of strings hanging from the waist in front, and behind with skins of coyotes, deer and other animals. Hanging about their necks they wore periwinkles and sea shells; the Commander gave them beads and ribbons. The boy wore the clothing given him by nature, for all the males go around this way.

Before leaving that camping place, Crespí buried one of the Indian auxiliaries named Manuel Valladares of the mission at San Ignacio:

His death I felt with all my heart, for the good services he had done me on all the way, acting as my interpreter. Anima ejus requiescat in pace. Amen.

Later, Serra found the grave, in an area thick with grapes and roses, disturbed:

His bones were scattered; we collected them and buried them again. Either the gentiles or the wild animals had dug out the grave. Much water was thrown over the grave to harden the rocky soil. May his soul rest in heaven.

There is no assurance of his ultimate destination, but he has not been forgotten. A geographical place name of Valladares still appears there on the map of Baja California.

The trail then led down out of the foothills of the San Pedro Martir Mountains and crossed rather open and sterile country in the general direction of Cape Colnett, only a little more than a hundred miles in a direct line from the goal of San Diego.

No matter the difficulties of the day, the Fathers never missed an opportunity to gather in a pagan, but their efforts were not always successful, as Crespí indicates:

A heathen boy had been following us from the Cieneguilla up to here, and yesterday as soon as we had reached here he was joined by a heathen man of these parts, and last night both slipped away... for which we are very sorry, as he was of great help to us in finding watering places. The Commander had clothed him very well, we had started catechizing him, and I had already counted on baptizing him.

Crespí describes their march over a tableland and occasionally over hills easy to cross:

We...came into a very spacious tableland or plain among the mountains; beyond this we went through some low flat hills

running out from the mountains, not at all hard going but...where we met nothing but brush without anything else that mattered; nor did we find water or any signs of it...We saw not a heathen, other than their tracks and some beaten trails...we stopped and set up camp in order for the scouts to go out to see if they could find water, since the horses have had none since San León; nor, in our expectation of finding it, had we brought any...The scouts returned well pleased, as now the seashore of the opposite coast was nearby, and... they had found running water in a creek very close to the shore. They at once set about carrying two barrels there and all the water bags there were, and took the horses along, who were doubtless very willing to be watered.

As the march lengthened and the days grew more tiring, more desertions of Indian auxiliaries were recorded. In this same area, Serra tells us:

At this place, one of the ten Indians of San Borja, named Juan Francisco Regis, deserted. We found it out only the next day.

the plain of San Telmo

We halted at a very large pool of water—a most beautiful place to pasture many animals, possibly for the entire year—where there was much good land for sowing. We rested here for two days and saw an endless number of antelopes, hares and rabbits.

This was from the usually laconic Portolá. He and Serra arrived at the valley of San Telmo. The name, La Poza de San Telmo, was bestowed by Crespí and Rivera's company.

From the nearby hills Rivera had his first glimpse of the ocean, barely visible in the distance beyond the valley.

Here some day the Dominicans, who were to take over jurisdiction of Baja California, would build a chapel. The possibilities of the valley were easy to see, even to the soldiers, as Serra related:

Some of the soldiers explained to me how easy it would be to start irrigating the lower plain; they assured me that in eight days, working with ten men, they could drain all the water of the swamp and have the whole land under cultivation.

The sick soldier with Crespí and Rivera, who had been carried on a litter, was recovering. But more Indians had deserted. Until reaching San Telmo, for six days they had found no mescal plants to roast for food. The expedition had been following trails beaten down by the tread of countless feet. The information that seemed to pass from one area to another indicated a vast network of trails. It was here that Serra received news from a native indicating that the first half of the expedition may already have reached San Diego:

He told us how the first division of the expedition had passed there, and how some Indians had left from here and gone with them as guides; and that they were now encamped at a place near the ocean, and that there the Father distributed rosaries to the Indians, gave them clothing, and poured water on their heads...Both for me, and for us all, this was news that gave us the greatest joy. When we asked the man how far it was to that place, he said that it was still a considerable distance away. May God permit us to reach there.

ridge after ridge

Though travel was now in a northwesterly direction, they did not draw any nearer to the coast, to the worry of Serra:

Today we could see how much mistaken we were in believing that the peninsular sea was close at hand, for after all these days of travel we see in front of us ridge after ridge of high mountains so that the ocean to the west seems every day farther away.

Serra and his party now were almost in the same latitude as the mouth of the Colorado River, and Serra was puzzled over several references in the diary of the Jesuit explorer, Father Link.

Serra wrote that Link's diary insisted that the South Sea, or the Pacific Ocean, met the Colorado River and formed a narrow neck of land between sea water and river water.

It was general knowledge, however, that the Río Colorado emptied into the Gulf of California. Thus, if Link's notations were correct, a great inland extension of the ocean lay somewhere before them and perhaps cutting off their advance

to the north on the route they were taking.

Serra indulged in speculation that this inland extension of the sea, if it existed, might be the Strait of Anian, which navigators had sought for centuries. In earlier times such a strait was believed to connect the Atlantic Ocean with the South Sea, or Pacific Ocean:

If this inlet of the sea were really to be the famous strait sought for in these parts for centuries, and not an expanse of land, but an arm of the sea, then the trip to Monterey by land should be thought of, not in terms of hardships, but in terms of the impossible.

The reason is simple. If the strait, as they describe it and try to discover it, goes from sea to sea, it is clear that not all the detours in the world by land would ever allow us to cross it, and proceed ahead.

Serra decided to leave final resolution of the question to the future. In the three days since leaving San Telmo they had passed San Rafael and along a route which follows the modern-day paved road to a point north of San Vicente.

the hills of Ensenada

Though the first half of the long journey was near an end, Rivera and Crespí wandered for eight days in the mountains on the approach to Ensenada, seventy miles south of San Diego. Portolá and Serra, in taking the same route, wasted the better part of six days.

After leaving San Vicente, Crespí says they traveled about a league through gorges and over medium-sized hills:

On going up the last hill to its highest point...we stopped for a while, looking at the sea on the opposite coast, about a quarter league away from us; and intended to go down to take the way along the shore; but seeing no way along it because of the cliffs, and the mountains all high and dry with no sign that there might be water in them, we took our way down through a hollow and camped upon a tableland.

That night, as they went into the mountains that lay between them and Ensenada, another Indian died, and Cañizares noted that all of them were threatened with death from thirst. They went in and out of various valleys, where they might locate water. On the third day from a height they again sighted the ocean. The next night, the animals stampeded twice. The next day it rained, and they were unable to travel. A mule was found wounded by an arrow. Again it rained, and the frightened animals stampeded that night three times.

Scouts were unable to find a road and on the seventh day they found themselves completely surrounded by the sierra. Finally, in despair, Rivera sent Cañizares out with the scouts and they as last found a way to a bay which he thought surely must be the Todos Santos described by the pilot Cabrera Bueno. Todos Santos is the bay at Ensenada.

Portolá and Serra fought their way through the same hills, though Serra related:

At one fell swoop nine Indians who belonged to our company deserted...questioning those who still remained as to the cause ...seeing that they were always given food and good treatment...the answer we got was this: that they did not know, but they rather suspected that, being near San Diego, they were afraid they would be forced to stay there without hope of returning to their own missions.

Coming down out of the hills Serra found the land heavy with large rocks and though it was late in the season, still strangely colorful with flowers and greenery despite the apparent lack of water. But by now only twelve Indians remained with Portolá and Serra. A few days later three more fled.

at Todos Santos Bay

A march of about eight miles brought Father Crespí and Rivera to the shore south of Ensenada on the Bay of Todos Santos. To Crespí it was a delightful place, all level land well covered with grass. However, as they had seen more signs of Indians than at any time on their march, Cañizares wrote:

When we went down to the beach we saw a large crowd of natives. This sight, and the fact that we had already suspected the heathen would be gathered on the shore, prompted the Captain to erect a temporary entrenchment around the camp site, using our gear for a barricade. We kept careful watch with six sentinels as a guard.

The next day, as they proceeded along the shore of the bay, Indians on a hill kept up such a clamor that Rivera ordered the guards doubled.

The two islands in the bay and the sightings taken by Cañizares left no doubt but this was the bay described by Cabrera Bueno and so identified on charts as La Ensenada de Todos Santos.

At the bay the Indians proved to be more curious than dangerous. As Crespí and Rivera continued around the bay they met Indians who gave them fish and mussels which they obtained with the use of little tule canoes, and who danced for their entertainment and begged them to remain for another night.

When Portolá came through he received information from the same Indians indicating that the ships of the expedition as well as the first section of the land party had reached San Diego:

Some of the natives came and one of them made signs that he had come across other people, indicating that in twelve days we could reach the place where they had halted and were living in houses and that there were other people in that place. This served to cheer us as we understood from the chief that the ships were there.

His companion, Serra, was delighted with Ensenada and its abundance of marine life:

As a matter of fact this space is just waiting for a mission; what with its nearness to the ocean, its level stretch of beach and its fine bay, it would be situated wonderfully well to ship in and out produce and commodities of all kinds.

81

the Coronado Islands

Since yesterday everyone excepting the Father, because of the lack of provisions, was put on such limited rations that there was only enough food to prevent fainting. Each person was alloted eight ounces of fluid made into two tortillas daily.

Thus Cañizares, the diarist for Rivera, divulges the hardships encountered by the first section of the land expedition after it left the Bay of Ensenada and neared its goal.

For a week they worked slowly northward, along the way climbing in and out of the valleys of the Guadalupe and Descanso rivers, which they thought would be good sites for missions. The Dominicans later placed missions in these valleys.

At Descanso the Indians were so numerous they could not be counted, and Crespí said:

Here they again told us of two ships, and that it was not much farther to where they had stopped; that there were people like us, with Fathers as well (taking hold of my habit and pointing to me). And so it was, for we were shortly to have our wishes fulfilled.

Serra later described the Indians in this area as tall and robust and said they would make Grenadier Guards for the Governor:

One of them thought it would be amusing to give me her baby, a nursing child, to hold for a while. And so I held it sincerely wishing to baptize it before giving it back to its mother.

On their way to San Diego Crespí and Rivera generally followed the coastal route of the modern highway and could see the offshore islands discovered by Juan Rodríguez Cabrillo and renamed later by Vizcaíno. On May 12, Cañizares recorded camping near pools of water:

We made camp near the seashore and recognized the islands, which we had seen from a distance, to be the Coronados... therefore we estimated that we were eight leagues from the Port of San Diego.

Crespí called the site where they camped, north of Rosarito and about ten miles below the present international border, the Pool of the Holy Martrys. Because it was closed by high hills, Serra named it Carcel de San Pedro, or the Prison of Saint Peter. The site is now known as Tahiti Beach.

behold California!

From a little height on this plain, we made out that the sea ran far inland; and in it we caught sight of the ships' mainmasts, scarcely visible from the distance they were at. I do not know how to tell the happiness and joy we all felt at seeing the hour arrive of our reaching the long-wished-for harbor of San Diego, or at seeing in it his Majesty's packetboats the San Carlos *and the* San Antonio.

Thus Crespí describes how he and his companion soldiers first sighted San Diego from the high mesa lying just below the present international border, on May 13, 1769.

Six weeks later came Serra and Portolá. They rode past one Indian village after another and saw a native dressed in blue cloth approaching. Serra wrote:

As this was something of a phenomenon here where a thread of cloth had never yet been seen, his arrival was awaited with impatience. From the signs he made we all guessed he brought good news. And so it was. He told us he had come from San Diego, where they had given him the clothes; and that if it had taken two days to come, it was because he had spent some of his time fishing.

He gave us an account of everything, although many details he reported seemed to us unbelievable; as, for example, that the two boats were there, and so many Fathers. But what gave us the greatest joy was that he had met, on the road, the Sergeant and his companion.

The Sergeant was Francisco Ortega, who had gone ahead to scout the road. Soon Ortega rode up with ten mounted soldiers from the first section of the expedition. By order of Captain Rivera they had come from San Diego with fresh mounts for the Governor and his staff and with letters from the other Fathers for Serra.

Serra described the final march that also brought him and Portolá to the mesa, though along a route nearer to the sea than the one taken by Rivera and Crespí. He was to write to his friend Palóu that the land was beautiful to behold and did not belie its reputation.

Portolá, however, had little to say about the climax of their hundreds of miles of marching:

We proceeded for about four hours along the beach. We halted on the neck of land of the Port of San Diego.

Diarios del P.^r fr.

Junipero Serra, i. Pr Juan

crespi.

Cax. 5. Leg. 6. n. 13.
8

1769

...but not the dead

All sections of the Sacred Expedition soon were united.

On his first night in Alta California Crespí camped near the Tia Juana River which crosses the present border before emptying into the ocean. The next day, when he joined Rivera, who had gone on ahead, he found a serious situation.

A camp had been established on the east shore of the bay, but it was a hospital more than anything else. The *San Carlos* and the *San Antonio* were anchored as near as the depth of water permitted. Already twenty-one sailors and a few soldiers had died, either of scurvy or of some unidentified plague. Many of the rest of the men who had come by sea were ill.

The first concern of Rivera, as second in command to Portolá, who had not yet arrived, was to find a more suitable camping place which would afford better protection and more access to water in the San Diego River.

After scouting the bay front, he ordered the camp moved to a small hill rising from the bed of the river at the northeast end of the bay. Huts and a barricade were erected and the sick moved by May 17th.

Six weeks later came Portolá and Serra. Portolá rushed ahead from a point below the present border. Serra went more slowly and also found a camping place in San Diego County, at the Otay River. He reached the hill, now known as Presidio Hill, about noon the next day, July 1.

There, he wrote, he met all who had come before him, "but not the dead." His section of the expedition had not suffered from hunger or from exhaustion, as had the others:

Thus was our arrival, with all in good health, happy and content, thanks be to God, at the famous and wished for Port of San Diego.

By this time, all of the crew of the *San Carlos,* except for one sailor and a cook, had died, and of those who had come on the *San Antonio* eight had died and all the rest were ill. At least three of the Catalan volunteers also had succumbed. But by July 3 a temporary mission was being erected on Presidio Hill.

Though it was July the weather was cold and Serra felt the need of warmer garments. The San Diego River had run heavily into middle June. When the ships had reached the port snow still covered the distant mountains.

Serra refused to concede to obstacles or tragedy. He wrote in his diary that he was surrounded by pagans in need of conversion and a "harvest of souls might easily be gathered into the bosom of our Holy Mother, the Church."

His diary, bound with a copy of Crespí's draft diaries of the Portolá Expedition to Monterey is in the Mexican National Archives.

CHAPTER III *The Promise*

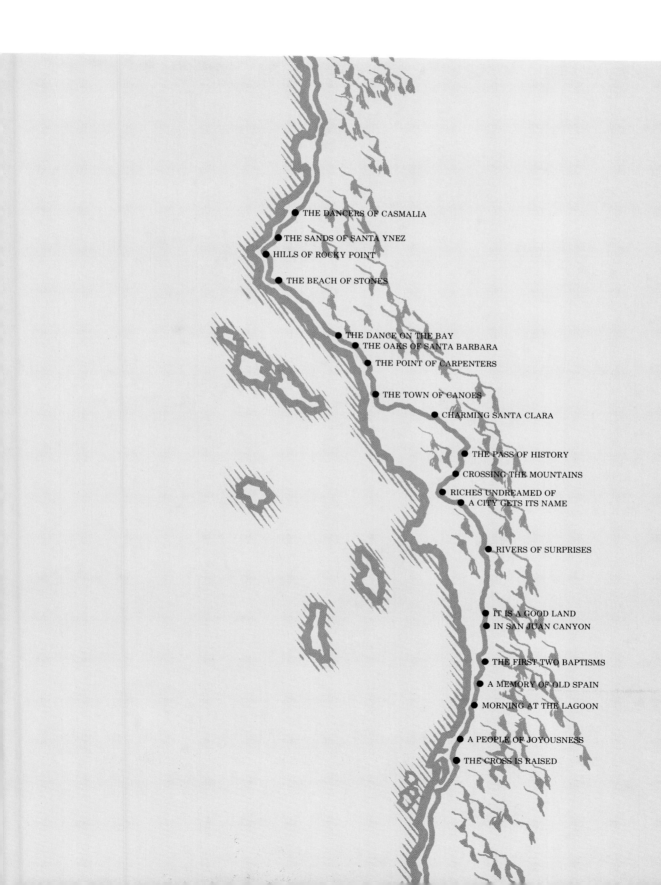

The cross is raised

It had been commanded that the Sacred Expedition should proceed as quickly as possible to Monterey. Portolá ordered the *San Antonio* to return to Mexico and report what had happened at San Diego. The *San Carlos,* for lack of a crew, was to remain at San Diego.

On July 14, Portolá was ready to resume the march to the north. From the ships he had received enough supplies to load 163 mules and he was anxious to reach his goal before the winter set in and snow could block their passage through the mountains that might lie ahead of them.

With him would go Rivera, Lieutenant Pedro Fages, and Miguel Costansó, the cartographer, who was to map the ports; some surviving Catalan volunteers, Sergeant Ortega and twenty-six leather-jacket soldiers, seven muleteers, two orderlies, the two Fathers, Crespí and Francisco Gómez, who had come by sea, and a number of Baja California Indians, a long train of seventy-four persons in all.

Left at San Diego were Serra, two other Fathers, Juan Vizcaíno and Fernando Parrón, and a handful of well soldiers, a number of workmen, and some Indians to help care for the sick.

Serra's diary was broken off. That of Cañizares came to an end. New ones would be written on the march north.

As Portolá's force marched away in the afternoon, Costansó began his diary and later noted the appearance of the leather-jackets whose equipment and mode of riding would leave a heritage for the later Western cowboy:

Their offensive arms are the lance, which they handle adroitly on horseback, the broadsword and the short musket, which they carry securely fastened in its case. They are men of great fortitude and patience...and we do not hesitate to say that they are the best horsemen in the world.

Two days after Portolá had left, on July 16, a cross was raised on Presidio Hill just above the wooded river and the Indian village of Cosoy, or Kosi. Serra preached the first sermon establishing the mission and the first Christian settlement of New California.

His words have not come down to California. Later, he did write in a letter:

Above all, let those who are to come here as missionaries not imagine that they are coming for any other purpose but to endure hardships for the love of God and for the salvation of souls, for in far-off places such as these, where there is no way for the old missions to help the new ones because of the great distance between them, the presence of pagans, and the lack of communication by sea, it will be necessary in the beginning to suffer many real privations. However, all things are sweet to a lover.

a people of joyousness

We set out from this Port of San Diego ...about four in the afternoon. We went northwest, over level land well covered with grass, near some inlets with salines holding very fine white salt.

This was Crespí's first comment on the resuming of the long journey on July 14th. Portolá's march led out past Mission Bay, through Rose Canyon, across the Miramar mesa, through Sorrento Valley, behind Del Mar and then to the San Dieguito Valley. The land was thick with Indians. Crespí remarked on their large villages of well-built houses and the presence of pots and jugs of baked clay.

They saw very few trees but water was plentiful in large pools, indicating the year had been a wet one. Of the broad Miramar Mesa on the way to Sorrento Valley, Crespí wrote:

We saw seven antelope running together on these tablelands, and at every moment we noted hares and rabbits running about ...we came to a very beautiful little valley, or hollow, which, seen from the way down off the tablelands, seemed to be nothing less than a cultivated cornfield, for its greenness.

They were passing through the territory of the Indians who in the mission period became identified as the Diegueños, who were a branch of the Yuman people. Crespí wrote of Sorrento Valley:

On a small height in this valley we saw a good-sized village of heathen with little straw houses. Upon hearing us, all of them came out, well pleased, to meet us.

In view on their right were the Peninsular Ranges which at some places were to crowd in upon the coastal plain. At San Dieguito, they found the valley rich with pasture, many wild grapes and other herbs. Despite the easy country, progress of the long train was slow. On the third day they passed across Rancho Santa Fe and through Green Valley and reached a large Indian village. Crespí wrote:

As soon as the camp was set up the whole village...came down. Their chief made us a harangue, and when it was concluded, they sat down as though they had always dealt with us—unarmed and wearing no paint. One of the heathen came smoking a pipe of baked clay, very well made.

morning at the lagoon

The explorers who had come up from Baja California described this new land as "mellow." They kept fairly close to the coast, because of the mountains which slowly rose to the east, though somewhat inland to find pools of fresh water and to avoid the frequent estuaries.

They camped the night of July 16 near where San Marcos Creek flows into Batiquitos Lagoon, which in the morning so often is shrouded in whispy mist.

On their way north they came to the end of the country of the Diegueño Indians and entered the territory of those who became known as Luiseños, who were members of the great Shoshonean linguistic family.

They came to the San Luis Rey Valley, and Crespí wrote:

Shortly after reaching here, we saw a long file of heathens coming up from one end of the plain. They came near the camp, forty naked heathens all painted over with all colors...The women all went decently covered, with thick bunches of strings in front and an animal hide in back; these came up with their bodies covered by a sort of blanket or mantlet that they wear from the neck downward, made of hare and rabbit skins twisted so that they fit very well together, and they can cover as much of the body as they wish with it. These women wore the mantlet so long that they were covered to the ankles, so well clothed that none of their body was to be seen.

The next morning, Crespí recounted, the Indians came back and his companion, Father Francisco Gómez, took the crucifix over to them:

...to talk of God to them by signs, how God had created the Heaven, the earth, and all things, both ourselves and them; and that Our Lord had died for everyone, so that we should go to Heaven and not be damned; and by their sign-making it seemed they must have understood some of it, and they made him a long discourse.

By now they were approaching a small mountain range, the Santa Margarita, which ran down to the ocean shore. They turned farther inland to find a road to the north. Their next camp was made at a river, which Crespí described as a good stream, and it was named Santa Margarita.

a memory of old Spain

The land was mellow and it also was fragrant. Never a day went by but that the explorers of Alta California did not mention flowers and trees and wild fruits. While at San Diego, Serra wrote:

There are so many vines grown by nature and without human help that it would mean little expense to follow the good example of our good father Noe (Noah).

The day Portolá and Crespí began the march toward Monterey they wrote of some willows, sycamores, cottonwoods, and live oaks. There were not many — but how different was it all from so much of the land with which they had been acquainted.

It was while they were still in Baja California, however, that they had first noticed the abundance of what they called the Rose of Castile, a little wild pink rose that reminded so many of them of Spain.

The rose is found all the way to Oregon. It is not the true Rose of Castile which was imported later from the Old World, but *rosa Californica*, which is small, pale-pink and sweet smelling. Once in Alta California they saw them almost immediately.

While crossing San Diego County on the way to Monterey, Crespí wrote of Soledad Valley with its very lush wild calabashes, or gourds, and the many Castilian roses. To him it was the Valley of Santa Isabel, Queen of Portugal.

In Rancho Santa Fe they encountered woods of trees unknown to them.

In crossing east of Batiquitos Lagoon at San Marcos Creek they found a spring surrounded by Castilian roses, and Crespí gathered a branch with six roses open and twelve about to open.

In the vicinity of the Santa Margarita River, there were clumps of wild prickly pears. In San Luis Rey Valley again there were many wild grapes and spots which resembled vineyards.

In an area now within the confines of the Marines' Camp Pendleton, in Las Pulgas Canyon, the story was the same, as related by Crespí:

Near the water there is a sort of garden of considerable size, with lush grapevines and countless Rose of Castile patches among the vines, as if they had been planted there. As the heathens had recently burned here, the roses were spoiled, yet the rose bushes were shooting up again handsomely, and we still found a sweet-scented rose that I plucked; and we saw many dry rosebuds among the burnt matter. For such a delightful discovery, and having reached here Saint Praxedis' Day, we christened it Los Rosales de Santa Praxedis.

101

the first two baptisms

Sycamore trees cast their leaves on the verdant valley floor of Las Pulgas Canyon. When the Sacred Expedition came through here there were many wild roses.

Not far beyond here is another and similar canyon known as Los Cristianitos, a name given to it by the soldiers on the expedition. By others, however, it was referred to as the Valley of Los Bautisimos. Crespí told why:

The soldiers on scout duty told us on reaching here that yesterday they had seen a girl infant in arms that was dying. We applied to the Governor for two or three soldiers to go with us, and we two Fathers went to the village to see if we could find this infant, and baptize it if it were in danger. Although we did find it in its mother's arms, scarcely able to take the breast, she could not be persuaded to let us see it.

As well as we could, we gave her to understand we would not harm it, only wash its head with water, so that if it died it would go to Heaven. Father Francisco Gómez baptized the child, as well as he could with her clutched to her mother's breast; she was named María Magdalena, and I have no doubt she will die and we have come just in time that this soul may go to Heaven...

As I was finishing writing this entry, we were told of another little girl-child about two and a half years old that also seemed to be sick, but we were unable to ascertain if this were really so; in the end we went back with some soldiers, and found she had been burned and was very ill indeed, so that I took the measure of baptizing her, as Father Gómez had baptized the other. I christened her Margarita; God take both of them into Heaven. So, merely by passing by, we have gained these two souls, so that they may plead in Heaven for the conversion and reduction of all these poor wretches.

It was not until some time afterward that Father Serra learned that Crespí and Gómez had performed the first baptisms in Alta California. To his dying day Serra would regret this honor had not fallen to him.

in San Juan canyon

A little before eleven o'clock we came to a very pleasant hollow with a great deal of greenery and many willows, sycamores, live-oaks and other, unknown trees. In the hollow is a large creek with a large flow of fine fresh water where we forded it; a little below, the water spreads out and stands in some large tule marshes...We named it the creek at the Valley of Santa María Magdalena.

This was San Juan Canyon which winds west about eight miles to the present town of San Juan Capistrano and its famed Franciscan mission, and then down to the sea. Crespí continued:

Upon this day's march we came across two mines, as it seemed, of fine red earth, ochre, and a kind of very white earth, on some little knolls, and we passed nearly through the middle of them; it was plain they had been opened up by the heathens, for the sake of the paints that are their gala

and ceremonial clothes.

They now had been on the road in Southern California for ten days and were well into what is now Orange County.

Constansó, as well as Crespí, was interested in reporting the appearance of the country, and he told of the day's march:

From the Cañada del Bautisimo we came to another valley, to which we gave the name of Santa María Magdalena, situated to the north-northwest of the first. The road, although over hilly country and somewhat broken ground, was not very laborious. The place had abundant grass, and was thickly covered with willows and other trees. The watering place was very copious, the water held in pools among reeds and rushes.

In contrast, Portolá had little to report and wasted no time on descriptions:

The 23rd we proceeded for four hours. Much grass and water and many trees.

Indians became more numerous as the expedition crossed the Santa Margarita barrier and now was along the foothills of the Santa Ana Mountains. They descended a hill at times seasonally bright with the red berries of toyon bushes and entered a long valley. Crespí wrote:

Going down to the valley we shortly encountered two good-sized villages, where the women and children were camped under some bushes and we were not able to count them, as they were all packed together; with the heathen men all smoking very large thick pipes of baked clay. We greeted them, at which not one of them came forward, but they made us their usual discourse, no telling what they were saying to us, and we passed on.

This valley is known today as Cañada Gubernadora and it lies in a north-south direction. Later the same day, veering west, they came to another valley so full of large sycamores and live oaks that it looked to them like a fig orchard. This was Arroyo Trabuco which lies near the border of the hilly country. They pitched camp on a nearby mesa a few miles south of El Toro. Crespí wrote:

The soldiers on scout duty said that when they found this place, they had made out six islands from a high hill here. On reaching here, Father Francisco Gómez and I, with Lieutenant of Volunteers Don Pedro Fages and one of his soldiers, went up the same hill. We did not see the six they had spoken of, but we saw two islands clearly, which they say are San Clemente and Santa Catharina. This latter lay exactly opposite where we are; and about four or five leagues distant from here is San Pedro Bay.

The Channel Islands of San Clemente and Catalina were known to Pacific explorers and the Manila Galleon captains.

It was here that Crespí, the padre, met the Indians with whom he said he would be content to remain and to serve:

I have told them some things about God...and we have had them kiss the crucifix and the rosary cross many times, which they have done with no show of reluctance. There are some pretty, fair-haired little children, whom I had repeat the acts of Faith, Hope and Charity. These Indians alone have won my heart entirely; I would gladly have stayed with them.

the rivers of surprises

From a slope in the Santiago Hills east of present-day Tustin, they looked out upon a spacious plain which rolled westward into the distance. They said they could not see its end.

This was the Los Angeles basin—in time to embrace one of the world's largest metropolitan areas. Their march, however, continued along the foothills of the mountains that enclose the basin, in order to be sure of finding water, and they came to the Santa Ana River east of Anaheim. Though it was the middle of July, the river was running wide and fast.

The inhabitants of a populous village entreated them to remain and live with them. A short time later, however, something happened, as Costansó related:

At this place we experienced a terrible earthquake, which was repeated four times during the day. The first vibration or shock occurred at one o'clock in the afternoon, and was the most violent; the last took place at about half-past four. One of the natives, who, no doubt, held the office of priest among them, was at that time in the camp. Bewildered, no less than we, by the

event, he began, with horrible cries and great manifestations of terror, to entreat the heavens, turning in all directions, and acting like one conjuring the elements. To this place we gave the name of Río de los Temblores.

The original diaries do not mention Santa Ana as the name of the river and it appears that the name was bestowed by the soldiers, or scouts, and was inserted at a later date by Father Palóu in his version of Crespí's diary.

Two days later they were at the San Gabriel River. Portolá recognized the area as a good site for a mission. Costansó wrote:

We pitched our camp near a ditch of running water, its banks covered with watercress and cumin.

The watercress drifted with the current. Cumin is a small plant of the carrot family, used for seasoning.

There was another earthquake. The next day, July 31, near El Monte, Costansó said they experienced another violent earthquake. Portolá said they felt six or seven of them.

a city gets its name

We rested today, and the scouts went out to explore the country.

At ten o'olock in the morning there was an earthquake, which was repeated with violence at one o'clock in the afternoon; and one hour afterwards we experienced another shock.

Some of the soldiers asked permission to go hunting mounted on their horses and others to go on foot, with the intention of killing some antelopes, as many of these animals had been seen.

Costansó identified the antelopes as a species of wild goat. Crespí said the antelopes were roasted and he found the meat "well-flavored."

Their progress northward seemed to be blocked by the Transverse Ranges which cut coastal Southern California off from the rest of the state. These mountains run from the coast inland and bisect the Peninsular Ranges which they had been keeping on their right. They turned west and passed below Alhambra.

They drew up to the Los Angeles River. The river begins in the San Fernando Valley, where it collects the runoff of two mountain groups, and passing through a break in the hills, crosses the Los Angeles plain on its way to the sea. Costansó described it as a river of "fine waters."

They named it Río de la Portiúncula in observance of the jubilee of Our Lady of the Angeles of Portiúncula. Had they followed it, they would have found an easy route to the San Fernando Valley. They also took note of an impressive wash that joined the river at what is now the heart of metropolitan Los Angeles. This was the Arroyo Seco coming down from the San Gabriel Mountains.

That afternoon and evening there were three more earthquakes but Crespí wrote that it was the best place they had found yet, preeminent among all the others, and he wanted it to be "a very great and abounding mission." He wrote:

At once on our reaching here, six or eight heathens came to the camp...and brought with them two or three bowls half full of sage tea, with other kinds of grass seed that they use.

They all came up with bows and arrows, but with the bowstrings unstrung. Their chief brought...strings of shell beads...and ...threw three handfuls of these beads at each of us. Some of them came up smoking upon tobacco pipes made of baked clay, and blew three mouthfuls of smoke into the air at each of us. Then their chief made an address to us, and we all sat down together.

riches undreamed of

After fording the Los Angeles River they followed the base of the Santa Monica Mountains on the plain well below the Hollywood Hills which enclose the northern end of the Los Angeles basin. Costansó wrote:

In the afternoon there were other earthquakes; the frequency of them amazed us. Someone was convinced that there were large volcanoes in the mountain range that lay in front of us extending towards the west.

Crespí gave more details on why some of them believed there must be active volcanoes nearby:

When this area was scouted, the Captain told me that about a half league to the west of here, in a ravine, they had come across about forty springs of tar, or pitch, boiling up out of the ground molten, and the water runs to one side and the pitch to another; they saw great swamps of this pitch, enough they said to caulk many vessels.

What the scouts had seen could have been the La Brea tar pits, or more likely the tar springs formerly near the present Hollywood Freeway. Beneath them, in oil, was a wealth undreamed of by the Spanish Empire, worth more than all the gold extracted in the conquest of Mexico and Peru.

The Indians were numerous, as Crespí related:

They came out to see us, and as they approached began to howl, men, women, and children in no small number, as if they were wolves...We greeted them; they wished to give us seeds, but as we had nothing at hand to carry them in we refused. We went on, but Lieutenant Fages was in the rear, and on his coming up to them they also insisted that he should take them; as he like us had nothing at hand to carry them in...they saw he refused to take them; they threw many handfuls of them in the air at him, and cast the rest up so that it all fell on the ground.

They were drawing near the Pacific Coast once again, east of Santa Monica Bay, and searching for a way through or around the Santa Monica Mountains in order to continue their march to the north. They had not seen Cahuenga Pass.

The scouts who had set out to examine the coast near Santa Monica and the road along the beach returned shortly afterwards with the news of having reached a high, steep cliff terminating in the sea where the mountains end, and absolutely cutting off the passage along the shore.

This forced them to seek a way through the mountains, "and we found it, although it was rough and difficult."

Southern Californians are well acquainted with the seashore in this area where a road in later years was cut out along the base of high cliffs which from time to time send dirt crashing down to the sea.

In the afternoon of Saturday, August 5, they headed toward a point where there seemed to be an opening in the range and entered the mountains through a canyon formed by steep hills on both sides. This is presumed to be Sepulveda Canyon and through it today runs the high-speed San Diego Freeway.

They rode up the slope of the canyon and at the summit they looked down upon a large and pleasant valley. Costansó wrote:

We descended to it and halted near the watering place, which consisted of a very large pool. Near this there was a populous Indian village...They offered us their seed in trays or baskets of rushes, and came to the camp in such numbers that, had they been armed, they might have caused us apprehension, as we counted as many as two hundred and five, including men, women, and children. All of them offered us something to eat, and we in turn gave them our glass beads and ribbons.

This was San Fernando Valley. The expedition called it the Valley of Santa Catalina de Bononia de los Encinos. The valley, they found, was more than three leagues wide and they identified many live oak and walnut trees. Here they rested for a day.

By Costansó's calculations they were fifty-one leagues from San Diego. The league varied in length from one country to another, and from one period to another. But to the Spaniards at that time the league measured about 2.6 miles. Thus by Costansó's figures they had traveled 132 miles. The distance by highway today is 139 miles.

the pass of history

In the San Fernando Valley the expedition was visited by numerous Indians who came to see them, as it was expressed, "from different parts." Costansó wrote:

They had information of the appearance of the packets on the coast of the Canal de Santa Bárbara. They drew on the ground the outline or map of the channel and its islands, tracing the course of our ships.

The ships they evidently had seen were the *San Carlos* and the *San Antonio*, which had gone as far north as the Channel Islands in search of the port of San Diego, which had been placed in the wrong latitude by earlier explorers. Costansó continued:

They also told us that, in former times, there had come to their country bearded people, dressed and armed like ourselves, indicating that they had come from the east. One of the natives related that he had been as far as their lands, and had seen places or towns composed of large houses, and that each family occupied one of its own.

Their stories again hinted of how information flowed easily over a vast network of trails. The Spaniards had been in New Mexico for many years, and had penetrated southern Arizona. There were no expeditions from there into California.

Directed by Indians, the expedition left the valley up an obvious pass between the San Gabriel and the Santa Susana Mountains. This was San Fernando Pass, which was destined to become a historic gateway to and from Southern California.

They entered the country of the Chumash Indians. In the hills toward the coast, in the Santa Monica Mountains, there is a cave with crude rock paintings. Among the figures are four men on horseback — Spaniards who had been seen and depicted — when, no one knows.

At the summit of San Fernando Pass they were warned by the Indians who had been guiding them that to the north were four other even more rugged mountain ranges and a large river they could not cross.

The mountain ranges formed the great barrier which separates coastal Southern California from the vast interior valley of California.

The expedition scouts did find a way out, to the west and down the Santa Clara River Valley to the sea coast.

The Indians were described as good natives and very friendly and affectionate and evidently widely traveled. Crespí wrote:

Some people have come up here from the shore villages, and one of them recognized Father Gómez, Don Pedro Fages, and Don Miguel Costansó; he rejoiced at seeing the Father, embraced him, and offered to have him come to his village.

Crespí wrote that he found the valley charming and named it Santa Clara. They arrived at a village where an Indian wedding was in progress:

Here at this village was what we understood to be a bride; she was sitting in their midst much painted and decked out in their style with a great many different sorts of shell beads.

Costansó recorded a peculiarity of Southern California streams:

We traveled for three leagues through the canyon which still ran in the same direction—west-southwest. We halted on the bank of the stream which, at the time of our arrival, flowed with considerable volume, but, shortly after, dried up with the heat of the sun, just as the scouts told us they had noticed on the previous day. This peculiarity we afterwards observed in other streams; they flowed by night and became dry by day.

We reached the coast and came in sight of a real town—the most populous and best arranged of all we had seen up to that time—situated on a tongue or point of land, right on the shore which it was dominating, and it seemed to command the water. We counted as many as thirty large and capacious houses, spherical in form, well built, and thatched with grass.

We judged from the large number of people that came out to meet us, and afterwards flocked to the camp, that there could not be less than four hundred souls.

The date was Monday, August 14, and the place was near Ventura. The village was situated on a point of land running out on the beach. The people were the Chumash, who lived in the area of the Santa Barbara Channel and belonged to the great Hokan linguistic family to which the Yumans also belonged. Costansó also wrote:

These natives are well built and of a good disposition, very agile and alert, diligent and skillful. Their handiness and ability were at their best in the construc-tion of their canoes made of good pine boards, well joined and caulked, and of a pleasing form. They handle these with equal skill, and three or four men go out to sea in them to fish, as they will hold eight or ten men. They use long double-bladed paddles and row with indescribable agility and swiftness.

Canoes were sent to bring native visitors from the Channel Islands to see the strangers. Some of the canoes were as long as twenty-five feet and were caulked with asphaltum which seeped up out of the ground. More than 200 years before the discoverer of California had remarked on these exceptional people, as Costansó related:

We thought that this was the town which the first Spanish navigators—among them Rodríguez Cabrillo—named Pueblo de Canoas. We gave it the name of La Asunción de Nuestra Señora, or La Asumpta, because we reached it on the eve of that festival.

Large sweathouses, as illustrated, were common in the Indian towns of California.

For three days they rode or walked slowly along the shore, or over grassy hills, as they drew nearer to the low Santa Ynez Mountains which follow the coastline as it curves westward to Point Conception.

They came to another village, as Costansó wrote:

We traveled for two leagues along the beach, and pitched our camp near a temporary village of Indian fishermen, who gave us more fish than we could eat.

During the night, these people serenaded us with pipes or whistles; these were very disagreeable and only served to annoy us and keep us awake.

Crespí named the village Santa Cunegundis, and it was near Pitas, or Whistles Point. Their experience the next day was similar as Costansó wrote:

The natives of this village immediately came to the camp...bringing fish, roasted or grilled in barbecue, for us to eat while their canoes, then out fishing, were returning with fresh fish. These canoes...brought an abundance of bonito and bass, which they gave us and offered in such quantity that we might have loaded the pack an-imals with fish if we had had the facilities to salt and prepare it.

Again on the road they came to another village on a point of land on a little bay. They counted thirty-eight houses, some so large they housed a number of families. Crespí wrote:

From a distance it looked like a shipyard, since at the time they were building a canoe, which was still lacking the last plank at the top, and among the soldiers the place became known as La Carpintería. Before reaching it, in a little ravine a dozen paces from the sea, we saw some tar springs, set hard and steaming slightly.

Costansó was deeply moved:

This place seemed to all very suitable for a mission, on account of the innumerable heathen that inhabit these shores within a radius of only six leagues, and because it has extensive lands well adapted for cultivation and capable of producing rich crops. We may say the same in a mystical sense, as the gentleness of this people gave us great hopes that the word of God will bear fruit equally in their hearts.

123

the oaks of Santa Barbara

Though the Indians they met, or who were accompanying them along the coast, were, as they described it, "pleased and merry," they soon came to evidence common to mankind everywhere. Crespí wrote:

The heathens reported to the scouts that, not long before, mountain heathens from inland had destroyed two large villages, killing everyone, young and old, and burning their houses afterward. And indeed, on going about a league we came across the first village and saw the ruins...two and a half leagues beyond we came to the ruins of the second village, which had plainly been very large.

Costansó was not so sure of what had befallen the villages:

On our way we found two ruined villages; we could not ascertain why they were so, but we concluded that it might be the effect of the wars and quarrels that arise very easily among the natives.

Portolá presented his version of what had happened. He says the inhabitants exterminated each other.

For the first time they also reported coming across bear tracks. They encountered another large village of at least 500 inhabitants and Costansó said they were the most affectionate and good-natured of all the Indians they had met so far. Canoes that were out for fishing returned to shore and the expedition again was presented with loads of fish. Costansó wrote:

From the Pueblo de la Carpintería we marched to the Pueblo de la Laguna, distant three leagues from the first. We pitched our camp close to a pond of fresh water from which the natives...take their supply. This was the most populous of all the towns that we, so far, had seen...in no other place had we met natives so affectionate and good-natured.

The lagoon was on the northwest side of the present Santa Barbara. Costansó said the place they camped on the following night of August 19th was fringed by high hills and the canyon was covered with beautiful live oaks and poplars, and pines grew on the hilltops.

Before the sun set on Santa Barbara Bay they could see islands in the distance. They were delighted with the beauty of the country and the welcome they were receiving.

On a Sunday morning, upon resuming the march, Costansó wrote:

The natives, not content with making us presents of their eatables, wished, furthermore, to give us a feast, thus manifesting the mutual rivalry and contention between the towns to excel each other in gifts and festivities, in order to merit our approval and praise.

In the afternoon, the leaders...of each town came, one after the other, adorned according to their custom...painted and decked with feathers, having in their hands some split canes with the motion and noise of which they marked time for their songs, and the rhythm for the dance, so regularly and so uniformly that there was no discord.

The dancing continued all afternoon and the expedition had a difficult time getting rid of their visitors. They return-ed at night, as Costansó related:

They returned with a large retinue of clowns and jugglers, playing whistles, the noise of which grated upon the ears.

In four days of marching on the way to the area of Gaviota, Costansó said the natives were living in a more civilized manner than at other villages as many of them slept in bedsteads. They also had separate cemeteries for men and women and on each grave there was a high pole painted in several colors. Hair was hung on the poles over the men's graves and baskets on those for the women's graves.

The soldiers named their camping place La Gaviota because they had kill-ed a seagull. Three of the Channel Islands now were clearly visible. Costansó said they were San Bernardo, the most western of the three; Santa Cruz, which followed to the east, and Santa Bárbara, the most eastern. On present day maps the islands, in that order, are named San Miguel, Santa Rosa and Santa Cruz. It was at San Miguel where Cabrillo had been injured and later buried.

hills of Rocky Point

The expedition was barely making five miles a day, along the base of the Santa Ynez Mountains, and the end of August was at hand. In about a month the massive Pacific storms were due to begin forming in the Gulf of Alaska and sweep the north coast of California.

Though they were a little more than half way to Monterey, their goal may have seemed to be receding with each day. The difficulties they had encountered were nothing compared to what they had yet to face. They had little inkling of them as they trudged slowly on their way without the happy welcomes they had been receiving. Crespí wrote:

On going about half a league in view of the shore, we went up to a gap, and then down once more to flats of the same sort as before, very grassy and with good soil, ending in high cliffs upon the sea...On going two hours, in which we must have made two leagues, we reached another small-sized village of some ten huts...The village is about five hundred yards from the sea, and near another point upon the coast.

Here we set up our camp; and the sol-diers found a great many flints good for striking a light, and nearly everyone provided himself with some, for his gun.

From their camping place in the highlands above the beach they could see another point of land entering the sea, about a gunshot from the camp. Between that point and Point Conception it appeared there was a small, but good bay. The date was August 28.

Because of the fine flints available for their guns, the soldiers named the place Los Pedernales. It means flints and today the point is commonly known as Rocky Point.

Crespí, however, named the village San Juan Bautista, the next day being the day of St. John the Baptist's martyrdom.

The village in this area also was a poor one, and the natives seemed to be reserved although friendly. The day before an Indian had slipped a sword out of a soldier's scabbard without the soldier being aware of it, and marched off. Other Indians who saw the theft ran after him and chased him into the sea, caught him, and returned the sword. They were rewarded with beads.

The expedition remained on the coast but its members had no way of knowing whether they could reach Monterey by this route. They came within easy sight of Point Arguello, which in time would grasp many a ship to a stormy and rocky end. Camp was made on the night of August 29 on the inhospitable shore of the point. Water was scarce. Crespí wrote:

It proved possible by a great deal of toil to get a little muddy water, enough to make tortillas for the expedition, but no water for drinking, except for those who had brought some from the last watering place...I named this hollow Santa Rosalía.

The soldiers called it La Cañada Seca, which suggested its dryness. After Mass the next morning Crespí tells how they followed a road to the northwest. The land between the mountains and the sea widened and was heavy with sandy dunes:

A great many heathens came up from some villages said to be nearby, and accompanied us through the dunes and sandy ground that still run on. After about half a league we arrived upon the full-flowing river here. The sea has it stopped with sand, and there is a way across between it and the sea water, so that the water of the river is ponded up and with no flow for a long distance inland; it must perhaps sink beneath the sand into the sea...In the dunes and sandy grounds here we have come across many bear tracks upon the very shore.

This was the Santa Ynez River. That day they had marched just one league, about two and a half miles. Looking east and up into the mountains through which the river flowed, Costansó wrote:

This river flows through a very beautiful valley containing many willows, and much land capable of producing all kinds of grain. We saw bears of great size, and many of their tracks.

They had now come more than a hundred leagues from their starting point on Presidio Hill in San Diego. Costansó's precise figure was 101 leagues. This works out to be about 262 miles. The actual distance by modern highway is 250 miles.

the dancers of Casmalia

They honored us with a dance, and it was the first place where we saw the women dance. Two of these excelled the others; they had a bunch of flowers in their hands, and accompanied the dance with various graceful gestures and movements without getting out of time in their songs. We called the place the Rancheria del Baile de las Indias.

Costansó wrote that they had left the sand hills to go somewhat inland and had reached the vicinity of Casmalia and camped at a large pond near San Antonio Creek. They were still in the territory of the Chumash Indians. The name of their camping site, Dance of the Indians, has disappeared.

While the pond at which they camped that night might not have been all that a scout had reported, another lake reached on the following day was a relief to tired travelers. Costansó wrote:

We directed our course inland, towards the north, leaving the coast in order to avoid the shifting sands of the dunes by which it is bordered, and other difficult places. It was not possible, however, to avoid a mountain chain that crossed our way, and extended from the interior of the country; but the sandy ground did not last long. We then proceeded over high hills, and through canyons containing very good soil and good pasture.

We pitched our camp in a large valley, near a lake of great extent containing fresh water—it must have been some two thousand yards long, and as much as five hundred wide, possibly more in some places. We gave to the whole valley the name the Laguna Larga. It is three leagues from the place we set out from in the morning.

This was Guadalupe Lake west of Santa Maria. The date was September 1. The season of favorable weather was fading.

CHAPTER IV *The Despair*

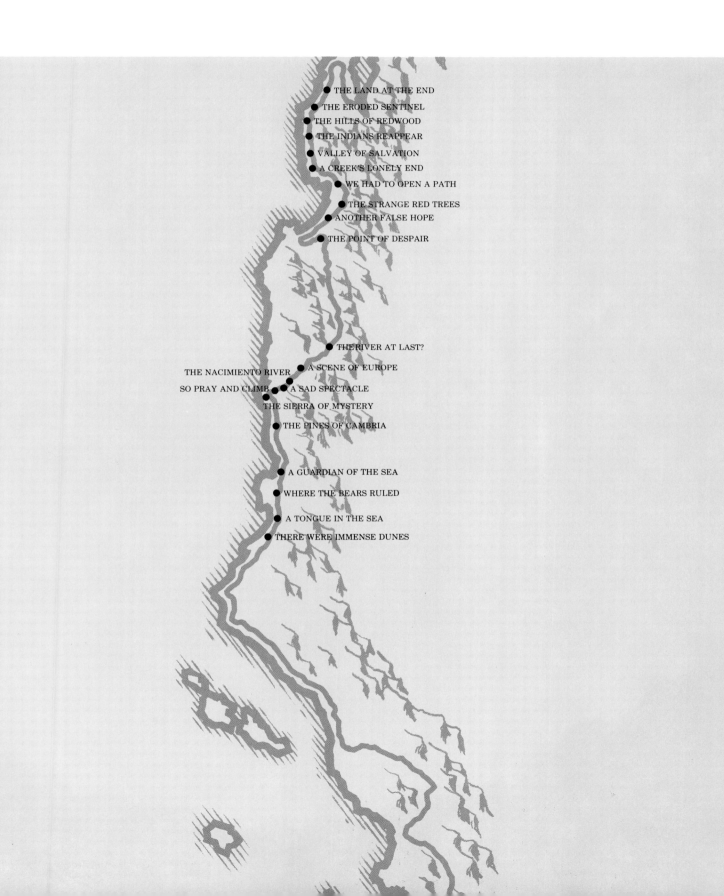

- THE LAND AT THE END
- THE ERODED SENTINEL
- THE HILLS OF REDWOOD
- THE INDIANS REAPPEAR
- VALLEY OF SALVATION
- A CREEK'S LONELY END
- WE HAD TO OPEN A PATH
- THE STRANGE RED TREES
- ANOTHER FALSE HOPE
- THE POINT OF DESPAIR
- THE RIVER AT LAST?
- A SCENE OF EUROPE
- THE NACIMIENTO RIVER
- A SAD SPECTACLE
- SO PRAY AND CLIMB
- THE SIERRA OF MYSTERY
- THE PINES OF CAMBRIA
- A GUARDIAN OF THE SEA
- WHERE THE BEARS RULED
- A TONGUE IN THE SEA
- THERE WERE IMMENSE DUNES

In the afternoon, as they had seen many tracks of bears, six soldiers went out hunting on horseback, and succeeded in shooting one. It was an enormous animal; it measured fourteen palms from the sole of its feet to the top of its head; its feet were more than a foot long; and it must have weighed over 375 pounds. We ate of the flesh and found it savory and good.

Costansó's account is the first of a killing of a California grizzly bear, which is now extinct. They were camped at a large circular pond they had found in a valley enclosed by sand dunes. This is in the area south of Pismo Beach. The soldiers called it El Oso Flaco, meaning The Lake of the Lean Bear, while others called it Round Lake Camp or Camp of Las Vívoras because of the presence of many snakes. The valley itself was described as wet, swampy and impassable. This was at the lower end of the valley known today as Santa Maria Valley.

They had encountered many difficulties on the way to Oso Flaco Lake. The scouts had lost the road in a fog and had failed to return until morning. The Sergeant, Don José Francisco de Ortega, had fallen ill and ten other soldiers were complaining of their legs.

The expedition was forced to remain in camp while scouts were sent out to try and find a pass through the mountains which were crowding in upon them. Costansó wrote:

The people and the animals rested today, and the scouts, who had set out to search for a pass through the range, returned in the afternoon, enlarging upon the difficulty they had experienced in reaching even to its foot—a fact we had discovered already by inspecting the country. There were immense sand dunes along the shore, and on the plain there were creeks, estuaries, and marshes, which formed a labyrinth.

The mountain range we had in sight is the same, in our judgment, that we have been leaving continuously on our right since we set out from San Diego; in some places it recedes from the sea, and in others approaches it, absolutely cutting off the passage along the beach, as happens at this place.

a tongue in the sea

They were coming to the rim of the country of the Chumash Indians. To avoid the marshes of the coastal plain they had gone over the sand dunes and then descended to the beach along which they walked for several miles. Then they turned east again, to cross more sand dunes and reach firm ground on a tongue of land between two bodies of water. One side was fresh water, walled in by sand dunes, and on the other side, an estuary which penetrated into the plain.

They were in the vicinity of the Santa Lucia Range, which is a part of the Coast Ranges and which had been sighted from the sea by all of the early explorers and the Manilla Galleon captains. Costansó wrote:

On the whole road we came upon only one small and wretched Indian village. This part of the country is practically uninhabited.

Near their camping place there was an Indian village and Portolá recorded that the natives there did not live in regular houses as did those on the channel, and were more docile. But Crespí wrote:

On reaching this place we found a good-sized village of good well-behaved heathens; they must have been some forty souls or more, camped beneath the lush sycamore trees. They were all very happy and well-pleased to greet us with a line of rush mats laid out upon the ground; on our arriving, eight or ten women who had been seated stood up, each bearing a large basket full of their seeds, and one after another went to and fro pouring them out upon the mats...What meaning this ceremony may have had there is no telling...In the afternoon the head chieftain came up with all the rest of his village...This...chief or petty king of this country is a tall majestic heathen...(and) is marked out by a great goitre hanging from one side of his neck, as big as a large swollen ox-gall, and therefore everyone called him the Buchón and this is now the name he is known by.

They were just above Pismo Beach. It was along here that they missed a route which would have lead them easily to Monterey Bay. They could have followed San Luis Obispo Creek to the northeast, the route of present Highway 101 which leads up into Salinas Valley. The long valley slopes gently down to the shore of Monterey Bay. Instead they continued along the rocky coast, the route of hazardous Highway 1. The mountains and the weather would be their enemies.

NORTH

WASHO

MAIDU

MIWOK

SHOSHONEAN TRIBES

MOHAVE

HALCHIDHOMA

YUMA

YOKUTS

KAMIA

COSTANOAN

SALINAN

DIEGUENO

ESSELEN

CHUMASH

where the bears ruled

The increasing numbers of bears and the thinning out of Indians indicated they were coming on different frontiers of Alta California.

After clearing a way through steep coastal hills they came to a canyon and saw troops of bears west of San Luis Obispo. Constansó wrote:

They had the land plowed up and full of the holes which they make in searching for the roots they live on, which the land produces. The natives also use these roots for food, and there are some of a good relish and taste. Some of the soldiers, attracted by the chase because they had been successful on two other occasions, mounted their horses, and this time succeeded in shooting one.

They, however, experienced the fierceness and anger of these animals—when they feel themselves to be wounded, headlong they charge the hunter, who can only escape by the swiftness of his horse, for the first burst of speed is more rapid than one might expect from the bulk and awkwardness of such brutes.

Their endurance and strength are not easily overcome, and only the sure aim of the hunter, or the good fortune of hitting them in the head or heart, can lay them low at the first shot. The one they succeeded in killing received nine bullet wounds before it fell, and this did not happen until they hit him in the head.

Other soldiers mounted on mules had the boldness to fight one of these animals. They fired at him seven or eight times and, doubtless, he died from the wounds, but he maimed two of the mules, and, by good fortune, the men who were mounted upon them extricated themselves.

For two days, now, they had noted, they had not seen a single native. Upon reaching Alta California they had encountered an almost bewildering number of Indian groups with varying degrees of skills and dialects. Their Indian auxiliaries from Baja California were of no help to them as to language.

The Indians of California were found to speak many languages and many dialects. The accompanying map shows the major linguistic divisions in the areas through which the expedition passed.

a guardian of the sea

Of all the places on the trail described in the diaries of the expedition none is more easily identifiable than Morro Bay.

They were following a canyon which turned steadily westward and after crossing a number of gullies came once again upon the sea. The land was pleasant with abundant pasture and quite a few trees. They were in front of Morro Bay. Costansó wrote:

Not far from our quarters there was a small and miserable Indian village with hardly sixty souls. They lived in the open, without house or hearth. They came to visit us, and offered us a kind of a pinole made of roasted seeds, which tasted good to all of us and had the flavor of almonds.

An estuary of immense size, which to us seemed a harbor, enters this canyon on the south side. But its mouth, opening up to the southwest, is covered with reefs that cause a furious surf. At a short distance to the north of the mouth, and in front of our camp, there was a very large rock, shaped like a round head.

At high tide it becomes an island, and is then separated—a little less than a gun-shot—from the shore. From this rock the coast extends to the west-northwest as far as a great point of land which we could discern terminating in the sea.

Between this point and another headland we were leaving behind, the coast forms a large bay, providing shelter from the south, southwest, and west winds, if it had sufficient anchorage.

The Indians described as being without homes may have merely been camping near the sea. Depending on the seasons many Indian groups either collected sea foods or gathered seeds and roots.

The next day the expedition followed the shore and found many pools of water which had run down from the mountains which at that point are only a short distance from the sea.

The place where they camped was given the name of El Estero.

Crespí, the padre, as well as Costansó, the engineer, took sightings as to their location. Crespí found the latitude to be exactly 36 degrees while Costansó said it was 35 degrees and 27 minutes. They were at about 35 degrees and 28 minutes.

the pines of Cambria

The mountains were beginning to engulf them. Crespí related how in four hours of travel they had encountered eight arroyos by which the water from the mountains ran to the sea. On the north shore of Estero Bay they were forced to turn up a canyon and they followed it for five or six miles. This is believed to have been by way of the present Coast Highway along Ellysly's Creek. The country they now were deep into was far different from the dry and hot land they had known so well in Baja California.

After leaving the canyon the next day they came to the top of some low hills to the northwest. Before them were the Santa Rosa Mountains of the Santa Lucia Range. Costansó wrote:

From this point we beheld the mountain range covered with pines, and a very deep canyon thickly grown with willows, poplars, pines, and other trees, in which ran a small river with considerable water, that some maintain was the Río del Carmelo.

They were not sure where they were. The position of Río Carmelo was variously placed on maps all the way from below Point Conception to Monterey Bay, and they had been given instructions to take possession of it in the name of the King.

However, they were on Santa Rosa Creek near Cambria. The Carmel River was many wearing days ahead of them. Costansó wrote:

We pitched our camp above the valley. This was named La Cañada del Osito because some Indians from the mountains, who came down to visit us, brought with them a bear cub they were taming and offered it to us. There must have been as many as sixty men.

The name meant the Hollow of the Little Bear. To the east, and lying between the Santa Lucia Mountains and the eastern hills of the Coast Range, was the valley that could have provided an easy path northward to Monterey. This route later became part of the Camino Real of the mission days. The point at which they found themselves at this time was considerably west of the present town of Paso Robles on the mission route.

the sierra of mystery

Not far off...we have a very high mountain range falling to the sea, that shuts off our way by the shore; this, and not the last one, must, we think, be the Santa Lucía Mountains... We have been lying by here in camp while the Captain and some soldiers are out scouting the creek and mountains for a way through, and to find where the way may need preparing.

Crespí, as well as the other members of the expedition, was low in spirit. For two days they had trudged across what is now the Hearst Ranch, along broken coastline, and on the third day they had taken a pass through some hills and then found themselves in a canyon at the edge of the sea near Piedras Blancas Point. This was at the mouth of San Carpoforo Creek.

They were only a short distance below the southern border of Monterey County, and nearing their goal, but fate would send them on for six more discouraging weeks in unfavorable weather.

Portolá decided to camp here for several days. Costansó wrote of the uncertainty of their position:

We thought that this might be the range known by the name of Santa Lucía in the sailing directions of the pilots who navigated these seas, and, particularly, by those who sailed with Sebastián Vizcaíno. Therefore, our Commander, desirous of assuring himself on this point, and with the object of exploring the land with the necessary thoroughness — rightly presuming that this would be the most difficult passage to surmount on the whole journey, as the old accounts dwell upon its ruggedness — resolved to rest at this place, and to send out the most intelligent scouts to examine the country completely, penetrating as far as they could without limiting the time of their return. So eight scouts, with Captain Fernando de Rivera, set out after midday.

The next day the explorers returned to report they had found the pass very rough and it would be necessary to use picks and bars to prepare a road. Late the following night the Captain came in to announce that the road was ready for the next morning's march.

We entered through the canyon which allowed us passage into the mountains, following it now on one side and now on the other as the lay of the land permitted. This canyon was very narrow; in some places the hills surrounding it were cut away at the foot, and were all inaccessible, not only to the men but even to goats and deer.

Thus Costansó described the unhappy climb which had been forced upon them by their failure to have found the easier route of the later mission days. The date was September 16.

San Carpoforo Canyon was wet with fog and heavily wooded. Some of the trees were unknown to them. In one day they traveled only one league, or about two and a half miles. They set out again on Sunday morning, without the Fathers taking time to observe an important date for their order, the Day of the Impression of the Stigmata of Our Seraphic Father San Francisco. Crespí wrote:

After we two had said Mass, we set out from the deep creek at the foot of the grade, and with God's grace commenced to climb this extremely high elevation, step by step and very slowly. When one had reached the top and turned to look back, it was fearful to see the depth we had left beneath us; and there was still a good way to climb, the most precipitous and steepest of all, and we greatly feared one of the mules might go over, to strike hundreds of yards below. At last we all got up it more or less without incident, thanks to God and our Father (St. Francis) protecting us.

They descended another very long slope and pitched camp in a hollow where some natives lived "without either house or home." Costansó said:

There could not have been more than sixty souls, a very mild and obsequious people. We covered, at the most, one league on this day's march, and we gave the place the name of the Hoya de Santa Lucía.

For two days the Fathers rested while most of the soldiers and Indian auxiliaries went ahead to open a road.

a sad spectacle

At last the Sacred Expedition came to the summit of the Santa Lucia Mountains which the early navigators had so ominously described in their sailing directions. Costansó wrote:

From the top of the hill we commanded the mountain range, which extended in all directions, without seeing its end on any side — a sad outlook for these poor travelers, tired and worn out by the fatigue of the journey, by the task of clearing rough passages and breaking roads through hills, woods, dunes, and swamps. The cold began to be felt; we had already many soldiers afflicted with scurvy and rendered incapable of service, the toil of which increased for those who remained on their feet.

They covered two leagues on the day's march and halted in a small and narrow canyon where there was hardly enough room for the camp. Costansó wrote:

The watering place was small; the water stood in pools; the pasture was extremely scarce. There were three bands of Indians in the immediate neighborhood — wandering people without either house or home. At this time they were engaged in collecting pine nuts, which the many trees of these mountains yield in abundance.

The scouts, who had set out in the afternoon to explore the country, returned with news of having seen a water course, and a canyon, convenient for the removal of our camp, having sufficient pasture for the horses, which were in great need of it. They likewise told us that the range was somewhat more passable in the direction they followed to the east-northeast, although it was far from the course that was convenient for us to take. They assured us, however, that the country gave signs of being more easily traversed farther on.

They named this place the Real de los Piñones because of the abundance of pine nuts and the large number of them which the Indians gave the soldiers.

The Nacimiento River

There was some relief felt when the scouts reported the presence of a water course and a more passable route through the mountains, even though it might cost them time and effort.

The difficulties they were encountering led Portolá to go into more detail than had been his custom. They knew they could not be too far from their goal, Monterey Bay, and that somewhere in the vicinity they surely would find the Río Carmelo for which they had been watching for weeks. Portolá wrote:

The account of Cabrera Bueno has good reason for describing the Sierra de Santa Lucía as being so high, rugged, and massive.

We inferred that we could not possibly find any greater range, as this was twenty leagues long and sixteen wide. We halted in a gorge where there was little water and pasture; here about four hundred natives came.

Portolá had no information on the higher Coast Ranges that lay just beyond the Santa Lucias; or of the mighty Sierra Nevada with their peaks of eternal snow.

The march was resumed in order to reach the camping place located by the scouts. This was at the Nacimiento River. Crespí wrote:

At about one o'clock in the afternoon those who had been out preparing the road returned, and we set out from here around half-past two, taking a due north course still through the same mountains. We traveled for around two hours, and must have gone a league, and reached what seems to be a river, though not a very large one…not far, they say, from where we stopped is its source…they say there are one or two villages of good friendly tractable heathens, and as soon as we reached here some of them visited us, bringing us pinole and good-sized pine nuts.

Again it was necessary for them to rest for two days to allow the scouts to examine the country carefully.

a scene of Europe

The scouts returned with joyous news, the first the expedition had heard in many weeks of marching. Costansó wrote:

They said that they had pushed forward for twelve or fourteen leagues, and had followed a canyon as far as its outlet in the sea...They believed also they had seen the beach, but this was still quite distant. Through the canyon flowed a river which they took to be the Carmelo, as they saw large trees on its banks—poplars, willows, oaks and other kinds. With this news the men were greatly rejoiced; they all bestirred themselves, supposing that the goal towards which we were marching was only a short distance away. With desire we anticipated our arrival.

The scouts, however, had seen the Salinas River which runs down the long and pleasant Salinas Valley to Monterey Bay.

Proceeding north and at times northeast toward Salinas Valley they came to another good stream of water. This was the San Antonio River. They were in Jolon Valley. Costansó wrote:

The whole country over which we traveled, especially from this stream onward, was covered on both sides with white and live oaks, as high and of as great girth as can be found in the finest parks of Europe. All the trees were loaded with acorns, as yet unripe; the crop would be so great that many herds of swine could be maintained. The Indians use them in making their atole—of which we have partaken in various places—and they also roast them, and eat them as bread.

On the margin of this stream there was a village of very poor, wandering Indians, but they showed themselves friendly and obsequious.

The next day they turned into Upper Jolon Valley. Crespí thought this land of oaks would be worthy of a mission, as one day it would prove to be.

Their hopes rising with every step, the soldiers and padres climbed up out of Jolon Valley and worked their way through a narrowing canyon and at the summit looked down upon the rich Salinas Valley with its shimmering river of water.

To the scouts it was El Carmelo. Near the present King City, after descending Quinado Canyon, Costansó wrote:

The whole plain that it waters is luxuriant of foliage. The soil seems to be of good quality, and produces a variety of fragrant plants, among others the rosemary, which abounded, the sage, and rosebushes loaded with blossoms.

From the diaries it is not clear just when the expedition began to have suspicions that the river was not El Carmelo, though it is evident they knew it did lead to the sea coast. But the scouts had been misled as to the nearness of the coast by the heavy fog. The enthusiastic words of the previous day vanished.

The next day's march took them down the valley and to the other side of the river. They noted pools of water with fish that they thought must have weighed as much as ten pounds.

Two more days they marched down the ever-widening valley toward the sea and made a camp at a place where they said the river was running noisily and swiftly. Crespí wrote:

Shortly after stopping here, not far off in the thick woods along the river...we heard a great deal of shouting and outcries from many heathens...The men went out and approached the place where they could hear loud shouting and clamor, and found many heathens, all carrying bows and arrows, who seemed to be hunting.

We supposed they had perhaps seen us and become alarmed; but this was plainly not the case, it was only that they were wrapped up in their hunting, and had not noticed us. We signaled to them with a white cloth to come near; they began to throw handfuls of earth into the air, and to play on a pipe, and the Captain said it was no use, and so we left them.

What is certain is that not one of them came over, or so much as approached us, and these are the only people who have shown us such behavior on all the way since San Diego; for all of them that we have met up to here have stayed with us and been friendly...and made us free of whatever they had.

the point of despair

A camp was made in the lower valley of the Salinas River and the scouts went expectantly forward to find what they hoped would prove to be the Bay of Monterey, and the end of their journey.

The date was September 30, and they had been on the road eighty days since leaving San Diego. They had marched 158 leagues or 411 miles, by their calculations. The distance from San Diego to Monterey by Highway 101 is 452 miles.

Instead of the well-protected bay which had been described by the early explorers they found an almost open roadstead. To the south, however, they did see a point which was thought might be the Point of Pines as identified by Vizcaíno's explorations. A rocky finger reaches into the sea.

Thus there was speculation that perhaps they had passed the Bay of Monterey because of the wide swing they had taken through the Santa Lucia Mountains. They were right on the bay — but did not recognize it.

Captain Rivera and the scouts followed the seashore southward. They returned to report they had found nothing but a small bay between the Point of Pines and another point farther south, with a rivulet of water that came down from the mountains and emptied into some small lagoons of no consequence.

This would suggest they saw Carmel Bay and its river. But, as with Monterey Bay, they failed to recognize the stream as the great river of rumor.

A meeting of officers was held. Formal letters were exchanged between leaders of the expedition and the padres. Portolá wrote:

I call your attention to the fact that we find ourselves today with eleven soldiers sick with scurvy — of whom eight are disabled — and the season of the year will naturally produce greater effects of this sort. The provisions are reduced to fifty sacks of flour, twelve packs of meat, and four of vegetables. I give this information in order…that with all the details before us we may be able to consult with greatest intelligence. May God preserve you many happy years. October 4, 1769.

The bay was thought to be in a latitude of 37 degrees, or even higher, while Costansó's sightings indicated they were at 36 degrees and 44 minutes. He was reasonably correct. The entrance of the Salinas River on Monterey Bay is at 36 degrees and 45 minutes.

Costansó argued it was necessary to go on. Captain Fages was convinced the bay was somewhere behind them. Rivera suggested the expedition rest and then continue the journey, as did Fathers Crespí and Gómez. It was so ordered by Portolá.

another false hope

While the expedition rested Portolá sent the scouts up along the coast to the north. They returned to report the existence of another river, and though the weather had been foggy, they thought they might have seen another point that could be the Point of Pines. Surely the Port of Monterey was just beyond the immediate horizon.

The impatient Portolá cut short the period of rest and the march was resumed on October 7. He was convinced that when they found the Port of Monterey they would find the supply ship *San José*. They trudged along the coast and passed over marsh lands. Camp was made near a lagoon where they saw cranes in great numbers, the first they had noted on their trip.

Their condition grew steadily worse and the following morning Crespí wrote:

After saying Mass and administering the Viaticum and Holy oils to two men who are dangerously ill among the eleven leather-jacket soldiers crippled with the Loanda sickness, we set out.

They came to an Indian village which had been abandoned, but because they had found several arrows and darts thrust into the ground, with some mussels at their feet, at their campsite of the previous day, Costansó wrote:

These signs of peace convinced us that they would allow us to meet and become friendly with them in their village; but the suspicion and fear of these barbarians caused them to desert it. This circumstance we all regretted, as we needed them greatly—chiefly to obtain information in regard to the country, and to accompany the scouts in their exploration, from which we hitherto derived great advantage.

They reached the "majestic" river which the scouts had reported. All hopes that it might be the Río Carmelo vanished. It was only a stream.

They found a bird which had been killed and stuffed with straw. To them it looked like a royal eagle. It measured eleven spans between the tips of its wings. For this reason, Costansó wrote, they named the stream Río del Pájaro, a name that has persisted over two centuries.

The world began to close in on them. They went north from the Pajaro River on a somewhat inland route to the vicinity of Corralitos Lagoon and entered the dark redwood country of Santa Cruz County. Costansó wrote:

We...proceeded for one league over level ground, not being able to continue the march farther as the sick were already exhausted, falling down from their mules. We halted near a small pond formed between some low hills—a place with plenty of water and pasture.

Crespí reported they encountered some strange red trees:

The scouts came back from exploring what had seemed to be pine trees, which they were not; but very straight, very thick trees of no small height, with a very slight short leaf; some said they were savins; but to my opinion they are not, the wood is red, and they are not junipers; they may be savins, who knows, but if so, they are not like any others we have seen elsewhere.

The savin, or cedar tree, was familiar to them from Middle and Southern Europe.

They saw the tracks of many animals and there was some discussion as to whether they had been made by buffaloes, and the scouts reported finding not far away some chestnut trees. The scouts were sent out once again. Costansó wrote:

The sick were in such a serious condition and so near the end, that, the sacrament having already been administered to several of them, we realized it would be exposing them to the possibility of dying on the road if we did not give them some respite and quiet. Our Commander resolved, therefore, that they should rest at this place...In order to save time, however, and to obtain information about the Port of Monterey, which we all believed to be near, he ordered a party to set out, and to advance as far as the animals—they were growing very thin from the cold—could go.

Four long days passed, while they waited for the scouts to return. When they did, they brought only bad news. They had gone twelve leagues and had not found any sign of the bay for which they were looking. Portolá sadly ordered the march to be resumed. They had left behind the Santa Lucias, and now to the right they would have the Santa Cruz Range, also part of the Coastal Mountains that they had been following since leaving San Diego.

"we had to open a path"

We marched very slowly so as to cause the sick as little distress as possible; we contrived to carry them on jamugas, as the women in Andalusia travel.

Thus did Costansó describe the resumption of their march which they forlornly hoped would return them soon to a more hospitable seashore. The jamugas is a saddle with an x-shaped back support.

They struggled through more of the strange forests of red trees and Costansó also referred to them as reminding them of the savin tree, or cedar:

We directed our course to the north-northwest, without drawing far from the coast, from which we were separated by some high hills very thickly covered with trees which some said were savins. They were the largest, highest and straightest trees that we had ever seen up to that time; some were four or five yards in diameter.

Another day passed. They came to the bank of a stream of good water. This was in sight of the sea. Costansó wrote:

On our road there were two bad cross-ings that had to be fixed. The first of these was that of a deep creek thickly wooded; the other, at a gulch at which a path was opened down and up.

Again, another day brought pain and weariness, in the crossing of a river swollen with rain water and the forcing of a path through thickets covering the bottoms of streams. The water reached to the girth of the animals. They named it the San Lorenzo River. Today the river runs through the town of Santa Cruz. On October 18 they left the redwoods behind and Costansó recorded:

We continued...over high hills which were steep on the side towards the sea. The shore is practically without beach on the whole stretch of two leagues over which we traveled. We were faced with three bad crossings, in as many hollows, which had to be fixed. These canyons had running water in very deep gullies, over which it was necessary to lay bridges of logs covered with earth and brush, so that the pack animals could cross.

a creek's lonely end

There was nothing resembling a protected bay on the section of the coast they were following northward on the same course of the present Southern Pacific Railway tracks. But they still were perhaps hoping that they might be on the shore of a Monterey Bay that was much vaster than had been described. Costansó wrote:

The march we made on this day was toilsome on account of the many ravines we came upon—there were seven or eight of them—all of which gave the pioneers much work, one especially because of its depth and the ruggedness of its sides. Into this fell the mule that carried the kettle, and for this reason the place was named the Barranco de la Olla.

The name meant the Kettle Ravine.

As was his custom, Portolá had little to report of the day's adventures:

The 19th, we traveled for four hours and a half, close to the sea; we had to cross several gorges that had been washed out by the rains. We halted beside a small river that flows into the sea. There was a village which, on our arrival, we found deserted.

The precipitous coast then curved more to the northwest. Costansó wrote:

To our right there were some whitish, barren hills that instilled gloom, and there were days on which we missed the comfort of seeing natives.

We halted on a very high hill and in sight of the white mountain range, which the scouts had discovered, where some clumps of pines could be seen. At the foot of the low hill, to the right and left, ran some streams containing plenty of water. Today we traveled for two leagues and a half.

They were at Scott Creek which empties at El Jarro Point above the town of Davenport.

By road San Francisco was about seventy miles to the north and Half Moon Bay about thirty-five miles to the north.

valley of salvation

From Scott Creek to Waddell Creek was not far but the weary expedition, even to begin the day's journey, had to break open a path over a ridge with picks, a task that required all of one morning. Costansó wrote:

We afterwards traveled a long distance along the backbone of a chain of broken hills, which sloped down to the sea. We halted on the same beach at the mouth of a very deep stream that flowed out from between very high hills of the mountain chain. This place...was named the Arroyo of Cañada de la Salud...From the beach a tongue of land could be seen at a short distance, west by north. It was low, and had rocks which were only a little above the surface of the water.

The point they saw was Ano Nuevo about a league from their camp, and they believed they were still on the great bay which they supposed must be Monterey.

That afternoon and night there was heavy rain, together with a strong wind from the south which Crespí said stirred up a storm at sea. On Sunday, Costansó wrote:

The day dawned overcast and gloomy; the men were wet and wearied from want of sleep, as they had no tents, and it was necessary to let them rest today.

Crespí also described their physical distress and the suffering of the men afflicted with scurvy. But also he as well as Costansó recorded a seemingly miraculous improvement in the condition of those who were ill:

We reached this creek with some sick men who were very gravely ill...After a good soaking they got from the showers that fell here, when we were expecting that two or three of them would wake only into eternity, instead these and the others all woke up mostly much better; wherefore we all called it the creek of San Luis Beltran, and of La Salud.

While they rested the scouts went forward once more on a reconnaissance. Crespí took the latitude, the first time they had been able to do so in days because of fog, and he said they were at 37 degrees and 22 minutes. Costansó placed their position 37 degrees and 3 minutes. Costansó was only a few minutes off.

For days they had traveled through a lonely but spectacular country. They had not seen a sign of Indians, who had been so numerous on the lower coasts.

After leaving the creek where the sick had been somewhat restored to health, they found their passage along the beach cut off by precipitous white hills. They went up into the hills and in a little valley found a village. Costansó wrote:

The Indians, advised by the scouts of our coming to their lands, received us with great affability and kindness, and, further-more, presented us with seeds kneaded into thick pats. They also offered us some cakes of a certain sweet paste, which some of our men said was the honey of wasps; they brought it carefully wrapped in the leaves of the carrizo cane, and its taste was not at all bad.

In the middle of the village there was a large house, spherical in form and very roomy; the other small houses, built in the form of a pyramid, had very little

room, and were built of split pine wood. As the large house so much surpassed the other, the village was named after it.

Crespí thought that the large house could contain all of the village's population, which he placed at about 200. The soldiers named the settlement the Village of the Casa Grande, or the great house. Crespí wrote:

They have a good supply of wood from a grove of savin pines like the ones we left farther back, and a good-sized creek of delicious water running through this small valley...not far from the shore.

They were at Whitehouse Creek which comes down to the sea near Franklin Point. They were entering San Mateo County and were encountering the Costanoan Indians who ranged up to the San Francisco Bay area. Artists with later expeditions by sea sketched the Indians who lived in the region of San Francisco Bay. They were painted and elaborately costumed.

The Indians furnished guides who led the expedition over high broad hills of good land, always and hopelessly to the north and all the time remaining in sight of the sea.

The land, however, had been burned over and despoiled of grass for some distance, but to the east of them they saw more groves of redwood trees of the Big Basin country.

They crossed three canyons and Pescadero Creek, and the latter had a fair-sized lagoon. Crespí wrote:

A grand place for a great mission, with plenty of water and soil; which I named in passing San Pedro Regalado. It is perfectly astonishing to see the amount of brambles all through here; they are a great hindrance to travel.

Camp was made at San Gregorio Creek, not far from the redwood mountains where there was another good village of heathen who received them with friendliness. Crespí continued:

As soon as we had reached this place named for our Father San Domingo, the whole of the big village at the place came over, all very well-behaved, fair and well-bearded heathens. The men all wore from neck to waist a kind of white tippet made of carded plants, from a distance looking like nothing so much as a white tippet open at the sides, with a hole to put the head through. This was all the clothes they wore, for the rest of their body was bare; indeed all the men hereabouts go wholly naked... Many of them carried staves painted in all colors with a great many feathers on them.

Only a relatively few miles had been covered in several days but a rest was ordered because the pack animals were tired. And the "miracle" of Waddell Creek was running out and they began to suffer from other ailments. Costansó wrote:

As the Captain of the company of the Californias, Don Fernando de Rivera y Moncada, was ill of the common sickness—the scurvy—and, because of a diarrhea which attacked many of us, we were forced to delay the march.

the land at the end

They did not know they were working along the base of a peninsula and that on the other side of the great bulk of the Montara Mountain, at the northern tip of the Santa Cruz Range, lay one of the world's great harbors. They did know they were entering a well-populated country. Crespí wrote:

Hereabout was a village of fine well-behaved heathens, who at once came to the camp and brought us numbers of dark-colored tamales made of their seeds. There must be villages all around this harbor, as there are a great many smokes to be seen.

The Costanoan Indians were members of the large Penutian Family, and the men in common with other California Indians went about naked during pleasant weather. When it got cold, they coated themselves with mud, until the sun was warm. The women, who tattooed their faces and did up their hair, wore short skirts, in front and back, made of deer skin or tule, and sometimes of bark fibre. Rabbit skin blankets were used as mantles.

It was Tuesday, October 31, and a cold Fall already was upon them. The mounting hills before them prevented further passage along the beach and a road had to be prepared to a ridge of the mountain.

From there to the west they could see a large open bay. The day must have been exceptionally clear as thirty miles to the north they could see a point of land which extended far out into the sea and helped to form a bay.

To the west from where they stood they could see seven white rocky islands of different sizes. The bitter truth had to be faced. Costansó wrote:

In consideration of these indications we consulted the sailing directions of the pilot Cabrera Bueno, and it seemed beyond all doubt but that what we were looking upon was the Port of San Francisco; and that thus we were convinced that the Port of Monterey had been left behind.

The point of land to the north was Point Reyes which helps to form what is now known as Drake's Bay. To the Spanish pilots, however, it was San Francisco Bay. The islands to the west were the Farallones which lie twenty-six miles west of the Golden Gate.

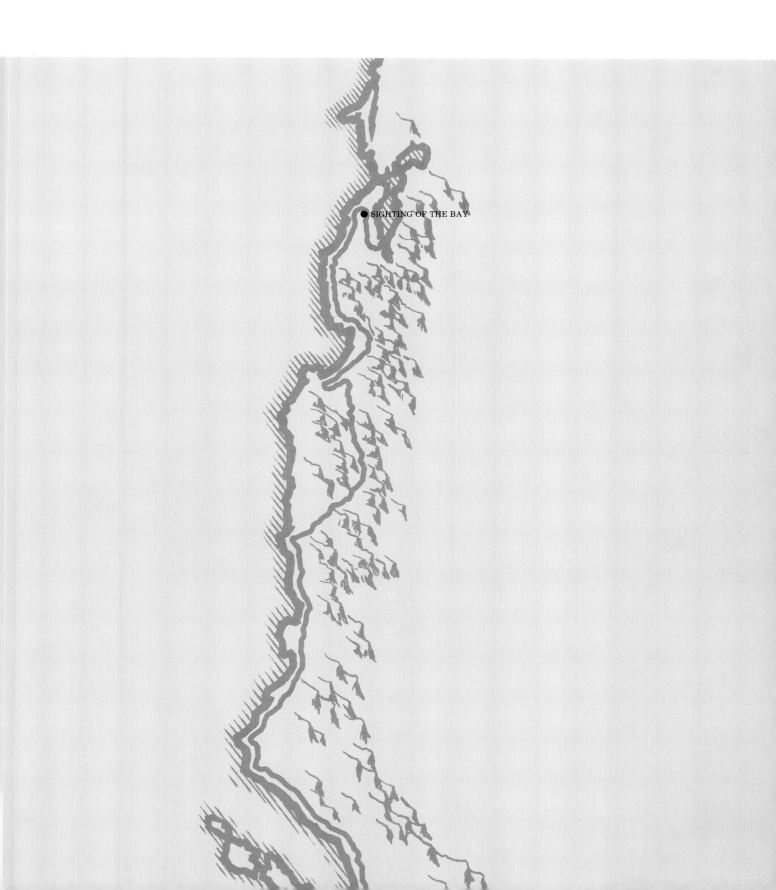

SIGHTING OF THE BAY

They had come more than a thousand miles—and their ultimate goal had somehow eluded them. They descended the mountain slopes and camped at the south side of San Pedro Valley in the present town of Pacifica.

Before ordering the expedition to turn back, Captain Portolá sent Sergeant Ortega and six soldiers out to explore the region, to remove, as Costansó wrote, "the perplexity of the incredulous."

That was on November 1. The next day soldiers at the camp received permission to go deer hunting. They returned after dark, and Costansó wrote:

They said that to the north...they had seen an immense arm of the sea or estuary, which extended inland as far as they could see, to the southeast.

This confirmed the belief they were on what was known as the Bay of San Francisco, as Cabrera Bueno had mentioned some ravines and that through the middle ravine there was an estuary where salt water entered without any breakers, and there they would find friendly Indians, fresh water and firewood.

But the pilot had been describing Drake's Bay and the long and only partially sheltered coast running down to Bolinas Point considerably above the Golden Gate.

The engineer Costansó put their position at 37 degrees and 33 or 35 minutes. The sailing directions of the Pilot Major of the Philippines for the Manila Galleon had placed Point Reyes at 38 degrees and 30 minutes, a full degree farther north, and Monterey Bay at about 37 degrees. Costansó wrote:

What is there to be wondered at if he places Punta de los Reyes one degree farther north than it really is, when he does the same with Punta de la Concepción ...and when, according to the same author, the Port of San Diego is in 34 degrees, when its indisputable latitude exceeds 32 degrees and a half only by some minutes?

In the evening of November 3 Sergeant Ortega and his party returned, firing salutes with their guns. Costansó wrote:

The reason for their demonstration of joy was none other than that they had inferred from the ambiguous signs of the natives that two days' march from the place at which they had arrived there was a port and a vessel in it. Upon this simple conjecture some of them had finally persuaded themselves that they were at Monterey, and they had no doubt that the packet San José was awaiting us at that place.

The *San José* had not even begun the journey which would end in her disappearance at sea.

Whether it was Ortega and his soldiers or the deer hunters who first saw San Francisco Bay is not known for certain. Historians generally give the credit to Ortega.

Heartened once again, the entire expedition set out again in the afternoon of November 4. Costansó wrote:

We set out in search of the port. We followed the south shore or beach of San Francisco until we entered the mountain range to the northeast. From the summit of this range we saw the magnificent estuary which stretched towards the southeast. We left it on our left hand, and, turning our backs on the bay, advanced to the south-southeast, through a canyon in which we halted at sunset. We traveled for two leagues.

The summit was historic Sweeney Ridge. From there the eye could sweep the greater part of the immense bay that lay far below, with its marshes and tidelands, and in the distance was another range of hills and Mount Diablo, a sentinel for those who would trek westward in the generations that would follow the Spaniards.

At this point Costansó estimated they had traveled 191 leagues from San Diego, or 497 miles. By Highway 101 the distance between San Diego and Sweeney Ridge is about 540 miles.

Portolá made no mention on that day of the great bay. On the following day, however, in order to skirt the big body of water, Portolá directed the expedition on a course to the south. Then he wrote:

We traveled for four hours...on a bad road and the remainder through a level canyon. Before us extended a great arm of the sea, sixteen to twenty leagues...which the scouts said formed a sheltered port with two islands in the middle. We halted without water.

For another day the expedition skirted the bay without being able to find a way around it. On November 7, Captain Rivera sent the Sergeant and eight soldiers out for another exploration.

Because of the lack of meat and other food, the members of the expedition had taken to eating acorns and most of them were experiencing indigestion and fever. On November 10, Costansó wrote:

The scouts arrived at night, very downcast, convinced now that the Port of Monterey could not be farther on, and undeceived in regard to the information of the natives, and their signs which at last they confessed were quite unintelligible.

They said that the whole country which they had gone over to the northeast and north was impassable on account of the absence of pasture, which the natives had burned, and, more than all, because of the fierceness and evil disposition of these people who received them very badly and tried to prevent them from going on.

The explorers also had sighted another estuary, or the northern part of San Francisco Bay, and there were no ships to be seen. It was evident they would have had to travel many leagues to go around the bay, and the mountains were rough and difficult.

It is clear from the diaries that they still did not immediately appreciate that they were looking upon a great bay. They persisted in believing that they merely were following along the shore of the estuary mentioned by Cabrera Bueno. In later months they would further describe the bay and assume that the San Francisco Bay of the early explorers had an inner as well as an outer bay.

Portolá convened a council of officers on November 11. Crespí wrote:

Early in the morning the Governor presented a writing to the rest of the officers, and gave it to us to read, requesting our presence at a meeting he wished to hold, to see what decision to take in view of the report given by the scouts the night before.

About nine in the morning the meeting was held, we two Fathers being present by request of the Commander. It was decided at the meeting that since this shows no indication of being anything but the inlet of San Francisco harbor (for we had very plainly seen the six or seven farallones within the bight we had just left), that this expedition should turn back, and we should go establish ourselves at the Point of Pines...and that the whole coast from here to there should be once more explored very closely; and once we were settled or established at the Point of Pines, if Monterey had not been found, that the whole of the Santa Lucia Mountains should be explored, down as far as the place where they had cut off our way along the shore.

Everything was at once carried out as decided at the meeting, and so on this same 11th of November this expedition set out from this place.

So ended the first search to find the Port of Monterey, in accordance with the instructions of Gálvez, the Visitor General from Spain.

On their return trip they promised themselves to make a further examination of the coast. Again they could not identify Monterey Bay.

Severe December weather detained them at the Point of Pines. Before leaving they erected a cross and buried at its foot a record of their journey, recording how in vain they had searched long and faithfully for the elusive Port of Monterey, and that they were returning, and they hoped, with God to guide them, to a a port of safety at San Diego.

Their route southward in view of snow-covered mountains was not exactly the same as the one taken northward. Friendly Indians pointed out paths they had not noticed. Portolá later recalled:

In order that we might not die meanwhile, I ordered that at the end of each days' march, one of the weak old mules which carried our baggage and ourselves should be killed. The flesh we roasted or half-fried in a fire made in a hole in the ground. The mule thus being prepared without a grain of salt or seasoning—for we had none—we shut our eyes and fell to on that skinny mule (what misery!)like hungry lions.

Smelling of mule meat, they arrived at San Diego on January 24, 1770. Their journey north from San Diego had lasted four months. The return was accomplished in less than two and a half months.

Altogether, including the efforts of preparation and the journey up through Baja California, they had been on the road for almost a year.

When Father Serra and Captain Vila heard their story and their description of the coast at Monterey Bay, they knew that the expedition had reached its goal and had failed to recognize it. Serra remarked to Portolá in despair:

You come from Rome without having seen the Pope.

In the spring, after the little settlement of Presidio Hill in San Diego had been firmly implanted, and fresh supplies had arrived from Mexico, Portolá in company of Father Crespí marched back up through California to the Port of Monterey, arriving on May 24, 1770.

Any lingering doubts they might have had about the bay were dissipated in looking at it once again. They found, too, the cross they had erected on the Point of Pines, and, oddly, with arrows stuck in the ground around it and sardines and meat placed before it.

Father Serra and Costansó arrived in the bay on June 1 aboard the *San Antonio* which had returned from Mexico.

The Mission of San Carlos Barromeo at Monterey was founded on the following Sunday, June 3. As Portolá said that the cross should precede the sword, Serra first erected a cross and formally established the mission. Then followed the act of taking possession of the land. Thus was California founded.

The offerings of the Indians placed at the foot of the White man's cross were symbolic of a land that had yielded a life of plenty with but little effort. The generations that would follow after Portolá and Serra and Crespí and Costansó would find that California was something different from what men had known before.

publication notes

The gathering of material for *The Call to California* required extensive preparation. Location of sections of the original Jesuit trail in Baja California was difficult and extended over a period of eighteen months. Most of the trail by necessity was photographed by muleback expedition that covered more than 500 miles. Photographs had to be taken at the time of year which corresponded to the progress of the Portola-Serra expedition.

Quotations from the journals of the expedition had to be significant yet correlated with scenes of California which have been unchanged since the late 1700's. Fortunately, much of California is still unspoiled, but for how long, nobody knows.

There were three areas, however, which were critical to a visual story of the expedition and which have been so altered by civilization that photography was impossible. Paintings of the three scenes, as they might have appeared in 1769, were substituted.

These paintings also provided an opportunity for depicting the uniforms and costumes of the expedition, the leather-jacket soldiers, the Catalan volunteers, and the Christianized Baja California Indians. This was done as meticulously as possible with the cooperation of Arizona Pioneers' Historical Society, and in particular Sidney B. Brinckerhoff, Assistant Director for Museums.

Most of the existing books on Baja California terrain and history were examined before a photographic expedition began its work in 1967. The best of Mexican topographical maps, it was found, misplaced settlements and points of identification, sometimes many miles, making it difficult to accurately place some sections of the route.

The publisher had the invaluable help of information collected over the years by H. E. Gulick who had planned, but never published, a detailed report on the Jesuit trail. Assistance also was given by Paul Ganster, a graduate student of the University of California at Los Angeles, who was studying the history of the Jesuit period.

Aspects of the route in California, which differed from the later mission trail, were worked out, first, of course, with the contributions of Bolton and then, in some cases, with more modern interpretation or identifications with the assistance of F.M. Stanger, Director of the San Mateo County Historical Association, and Don Meadows of Santa Ana.

There are several versions of the principal diaries or journals of the Portola-Serra expedition from which quotations were chosen.

In most cases members of the expedition made rough notes from time to time of their journey. The notes were filled out, revised, or added to later. Copies were made, sometimes by other hands, and in some cases the originals reduced, for various official sources or in the interest of posterity. Leaders of the expedition fully understood the importance of their discoveries and observations.

The diary of Father Junípero Serra used for this book is his original one which was found in 1945 in the National Archives of Mexico by Father Maynard Geiger, O.F.M., who wrote *The Life and Times of Father Serra*. Quotations are from *Writings of Junípero Serra, Vol. I*, translated by Antonine Tibesar, O.F.M., published in 1955 by The American Academy of Franciscan History.

Before this discovery, the principal

version of the journal used by most historians was an early copy made by Father Juan Vizcaíno, whose writing hand was paralyzed by Indian arrows at San Diego just before he completed copying it.

There are a number of manuscripts of Father Juan Crespí's many travels; for the expedition of 1769 there are two principal texts, a draft version and a final copy, both first brought to light by Father Geiger. Both versions have been drawn upon for the quotations used here, through the courtesy and cooperation of Alan K. Brown, of the University of Arizona, whose translations are as yet unpublished. Mr. Brown also read the manuscript and made a number of suggestions as to accuracy and surmises.

By contrast, the texts copied by Crespí's companion, Father Francisco Palóu, and translated by Herbert Eugene Bolton in four volumes, *Historical Memoirs of New California,* published at Berkeley in 1926, are greatly altered and abridged, with Crespí's actual writing heavily interspersed with material taken bodily from the parallel journal kept by Miguel Costansó.

Excerpts from the diary of Miguel Constansó are from *The Narrative of the Portolá Expedition of 1769-1770 by Miguel Costansó,* translated and edited by Frederick J. Teggart and published by the Academy of Pacific Coast History, University of California, Berkeley, in 1911. This version was reprinted in 1967 by the San Mateo County Historical Society.

The quotations of Portolá are from the *Diary of Gaspar de Portolá During the California Expedition of 1769-1770,* translated and edited by Donald Eugene Smith and Frederick J. Teggart, and published

by the Academy of Pacific Coast History, University of California, Berkeley, in 1909.

The translation of the diary of José de Cañizares, *Putting a Lid on California: An Unpublished Diary of the Portolá Expedition by José de Cañizares,* by Virginia E. Thickens and Margaret Mollins, was published in the California Historical Society Quarterly in 1952.

Wherever possible, photographs in the book show the country much as it appeared in 1769. In two cases, where such photography was no longer possible, historic photographs were substituted. That of the Los Angeles River, for example, only slightly retouched, shows the river as it appeared in the 1880's.

The colored lithographs of Indians of the San Francisco Bay region and of the grizzly bear are from the Carl Wheat Collection, Bancroft Library of the University of California. They were drawn by Louis Choris, artist on board the Russian ship *Rurik* in the Kotzebue Expedition of 1816, and published in Paris in 1822.

Other artwork sources: photographs of the Los Angeles River and Santa Barbara Bay, and sketch of an Indian sweathouse interior are from the Pierce Collection, Henry E. Huntington Library and Art Gallery, San Marino; photograph of Father Serra's diary, Archivo General de la Nacion, Mexico City; sketch of Diegueño Indian hut by John Audubon, Southwest Museum, Los Angeles; Spanish Map of 1768, Honnold Library, Claremont; English Map, Anson's Voyages Around the World; Vizcaíno Maps, California Historical Society Quarterly, December, 1928; drawing of Chumash Indians with canoe by Image, Art Division of Frye & Smith, Ltd., San Diego.

INDEX

This book was produced by Image, the Art Division of Frye & Smith, Ltd. Lithography by Frye & Smith, Ltd., on Casco Dull 80 pound text. Typography by Linotron, the Typesetting Division of Frye & Smith, Ltd. The type face used is 10 point Century Schoolbook. Binding by Cardoza Bookbinding Co.